Charing Cross to st . Paul's

Joseph Pennell

Copyright © BiblioLife, LLC

BiblioLife Reproduction Series: Our goal at BiblioLife is to help readers, educators and researchers by bringing back in print hard-to-find original publications at a reasonable price and, at the same time, preserve the legacy of literary history. The following book represents an authentic reproduction of the text as printed by the original publisher and may contain prior copyright references. While we have attempted to accurately maintain the integrity of the original work(s), from time to time there are problems with the original book scan that may result in minor errors in the reproduction, including imperfections such as missing and blurred pages, poor pictures, markings and other reproduction issues beyond our control. Because this work is culturally important, we have made it available as a part of our commitment to protecting, preserving and promoting the world's literature.

All of our books are in the "public domain" and some are derived from Open Source projects dedicated to digitizing historic literature. We believe that when we undertake the difficult task of re-creating them as attractive, readable and affordable books, we further the mutual goal of sharing these works with a larger audience. A portion of BiblioLife profits go back to Open Source projects in the form of a donation to the groups that do this important work around the world. If you would like to make a donation to these worthy Open Source projects, or would just like to get more information about these important initiatives, please visit www.bibliolife.com/opensource.

CHARING CROSS
TO ST. PAUL'S

NOTES BY
JUSTIN McCARTHY, M.P.

AND VIGNETTES BY
JOSEPH PENNELL

LONDON
SEELEY AND CO., LIMITED
ESSEX STREET, STRAND
1893

CONTENTS

CHAP.		PAGE
I. Introduction		1
II. Charing Cross		20
III. The Strand		63
IV. The Strand (*continued*)		104
V. The Law Courts		147
VI. Fleet Street		184
VII. Ludgate Hill		213
VIII. St. Paul's		238

LIST OF ILLUSTRATIONS

Chancery Lane . . . . . *Frontispiece*	
	PAGE
Flower Girls at Charing Cross . . .	23
Trafalgar Square	29
Charing Cross	33
King Charles's Statue	37
Morley's Hotel, Trafalgar Square . . .	41
St. Martin's in the Fields	45
Busses	53
Fish Shop at Charing Cross	59
In the Strand	67
The Strand	71
Exeter Hall	77
Terry's Theatre	81
The Gaiety	86
Wellington Street	89
The Lyceum	93
Burleigh Street, Strand	99

List of Illustrations

	PAGE
The Strand, by Somerset House	105
Somerset House	111
St. Mary-le-Strand	119
St. Mary-le-Strand from the East	125
Old Houses in Holywell Street	129
St. Clement Danes	135
The Corner of Essex Street	151
The Law Courts	161
Entrance to the Courts	171
The Clock Tower of the Law Courts	177
Fleet Street	185
St. Dunstan's in the West	189
The Windows of "Punch"	192
St. Bride's Passage	193
"Sporting Life" Office	197
"Daily News" Office	203
The Railway Bridge, Ludgate Hill	214
Ludgate Circus	217
Wild's Hotel	223
St. Martin's, Ludgate	231
St. Paul's Churchyard	243
West Door of St. Paul's	255

Charing Cross to St. Paul's

I

INTRODUCTION

WE cannot—at least I cannot, to put it more modestly—reconstruct in mind the London of the far, very far past. I have set myself the task often, and laboriously tried to accomplish it, but it will not shape itself, that far-away Roman London: it will not shape itself to my eyes or my mind. I cannot see the London with the cinctures of the great wall and the seven gates and the double doors to each gate. The historical suggestion conveys to my mind no manner of idea. I cannot get back to a Roman London —a fortress London; I can hardly believe in it. But lest any one should take my words too literally, and should assume me to be guilty of an absurd scepticism which ought to be instantly confuted by the citation of overwhelming evidence from history, I hasten to explain that I am not really sceptical in that sense. I have not the smallest doubt about the existence of the Roman London; I only mean to say that I cannot believe in it in the sense of realising it and understanding what it would be to live in it. I have a friend who only cares about romances and novels which tell of the time with which he is familiar; he will not condescend to read even the finest story of the chivalric age. "I don't believe in a man in armour," he says. Now my friend is, apart from this curious self-accepted limitation to his reading, a well-read man; he is perfectly well aware that in olden days knights went to battle encased in steel; I have no doubt he could, if need were, favour any company with a dissertation on the various kinds of armour in which men of different chivalric orders and ages bedizened and defended themselves. But his imagination does not realise the mail-clad hero as a living creature, as a man and a brother with a soul to be saved, and a heart to be perplexed and betossed, and in that sense he does not believe in the man in armour. In that sense, and that sense only, I fail to put faith in Roman London. It lives for history; it does not live for me.

I have somewhat of a similar notion with regard to Rome—a notion which I fancy I share with most people, even with some scholarly persons, if they would only acknowledge it. I cannot reconstruct in my own mind the Rome of the Republican days. In vain I read and study and survey the ground itself; no Rome rises for me but the Imperial Rome—the Rome of the Cæsars— the Rome of the Empire, or at all events, the Rome of those days which were blossoming or decaying into empire—the Rome of the first and greatest Imperator. I am inclined to think that it is so with most persons, and that the Rome which they can see in the mind's eye is the Rome which Horace and Juvenal and Martial and Persius have described for us. London is real for me only so far back as when she rises before me mediæval; I can see her, recognise her, study her, appreciate her, and even live in her as the London of Chaucer; beyond that day she is not London for me, but might be confounded with Troy or Persepolis or the capital of Cloud-cuckoo-land.

Of that mediæval London the most living, the most vital, the most real part, is that stretch of thoroughfare which connects Charing Cross with St. Paul's. In this volume the artist with the pencil—who plays a much more important part than the would-be artist with the pen—has taken from Charing Cross to St. Paul's for his province. This was, this is, the backbone of London. Mediæval London grew up around it. The Strand was the baldric which belted Court and Parliament together; the town grew up along and about the Strand as a coral island grows in the sea. Something of that growth and its gradual realisation is brought home to one's mind rather oddly during any session of the House of Commons. It happens in this way: A stranger standing in the inner lobby of the House of Commons at the moment when the House adjourns for the night is surprised to see an official rush into the midst of the dispersing crowd and to hear him shout, in tone loud as that of some Homeric hero, the mystic question, "Who goes home?" There is no answer—the man with the Homeric voice does not seem to expect any. The stranger naturally asks for an explanation. The explanation is found in the fact that once upon a time London and Westminster were separate and widely-separated cities—a sort of desert of barbarism lay between. But a desert is not necessarily a place absolutely unpeopled. The Eastern desert has its Bedouins; the desert between Westminster and London had its footpads and its mounted highwaymen. People made up parties to ride home together, themselves and their servants, for common safety. So the official of the Houses of Parliament had it as one of his regular duties to shout out in the lobbies and the corridors the invitation which called on home-going people to close their ranks, to form this or that group, and to ride together across the perils of Lincoln's Inn Fields, or close by the skirts of Alsatia. Now, when the times are all changed, when not one member of Parliament out of a baker's dozen goes Cityward on his way home, when the highwayman has disappeared even out of our literature—unless where perchance he still lingers and lurks in the yellowing paper and the blurred print of some mean little publication for boys—still the nightly cry of "Who goes home?" is heard re-echoing across the lobby and through the corridors, and even along the terrace of the House of Commons.

Long may it sound! May its echo never grow less! May no rage of modern innovation, realism, or utility abolish that function and silence that call! It keeps alive in our minds—in the minds of those who have minds—some idea of the gradual growth of

London; we think of the nightly wayfarers riding or driving eastward, and we are thereby reminded of the growth of the Strand, and the part that growth played in the creation of what we know as London. Do not let us assume too hastily that all since that time has been mere and sheer progress. We do not now make up parties to go home together for common safety, but might it not be well if we still sometimes did so? The highwaymen are gone, to be sure, but the robbers now occasionally—indeed, not infrequently—take to the use of the revolver, and I have heard travelled men say that there are few places which have ever really scared them of nights like the Thames Embankment. However, I am not now engaged in a study of social progress, or a comparison of the virtues and the vices, of the dangers and the protections of this time and any other. My concern is to point to the fact that London grew up along and around the Strand, so that he who fares with Mr. Pennell, and if I may say so, with me, from Charing Cross to St. Paul's, will have trodden the main highroad of England's national and imperial history.

Palaces grew up along the Strand—we must remember that it was then a strand, and that the few houses built on its south side looked on the Thames—palaces began to grow up, for the great nobles naturally liked to have houses not quite too far either from Westminster or from the City. The younger nobles, and some of the elders just as well, no doubt, were fond of going down into the City; the nobles borrowed money there from the acknowledged money-lenders, and from the jewellers and the silversmiths. The City wives had the repute of being pretty and coquettish ever since the days of Chaucer, and, perhaps, indeed, since long before: the young "swells" loved to go down to the City; the citizens' wives were not ashamed then to sell their wares openly in their shops; they sold embroidered shirts for the gallants, and gorgeous laced undergarments for the ladies; and one may fancy from the dramatic literature of the time that many a middle-aged gentleman professed to have gone down to the shops of the City merely in search of pretty gifts of lace and embroidery to bring home to his wife and his daughters. In the later Elizabethan days and throughout the time of King James the City became a favourite haunt of gallants who loved to smoke tobacco. They did not call it "smoking tobacco" then—they called it "drinking tobacco"; they inhaled the tobacco into their throats, and they, not unnaturally, called that drinking it. Then, when there were any great difficulties in the wars of the sovereign, when troops had to be levied and money raised, when foreign war seemed to become inevitable, or domestic rebellion was whispered of in the North or in the West, then the City became a place of signal importance, and the ministers of the King were none too proud to go there and stand, metaphorically, plumed cap in hand, and beseech of the City magnates to rally with their money-bags around the Throne.

The City was almost always devoted and loyal—always, indeed, unless and until the kings entirely overdid the business of sovereign kingship, as some of them certainly did, and then the City got together its trainbands and manfully stood by the country. But, in the meantime—for we have been anticipating a good deal—the City was becoming gradually of more and more importance to the King and the Court and the nobles, and so the stately palaces began to arise along the Strand. Many an ancient water-gate, looking curiously out of date to-day amid the upsetting and demolishing and reconstructing newnesses of the Thames Embankment, tells of that ancient time when the Strand was open to the river, even as the iron mooring-rings on some of the street walls of Ravenna remind one of the days when Ravenna was another Venice, and forewarn us of the days when Venice is to be another Ravenna.

The narrow belt of the occupied Strand began to broaden and to thicken; the palaces increased on either side, shutting out the river and the fields; then the houses began to jostle each other; the poor little Roman bath, stone-cold in its niche, got gradually blocked up and hidden away, and had grown to be almost as much of a curiosity five centuries ago as it is in our own day; the river was beginning to be more and more occupied by wharfs and warehouses; the Westminster quarter was sending its offshoots down along the line of streets; the City was sending its offshoots up along the line of river; the Strand was turning from the Strand properly so called into the Strand improperly so called—as we have known it all our lives, and our grandfathers and grandmothers before us. Between certain palaces of nobles and shops of burghers there ran green and pleasant lanes down to the Thames—then, and for long after, a silver stream, and in the season hawthorn still blossomed in the lanes and honeysuckle made them fragrant. This was on the south side of the Strand. On the north side there were glimpses of the fields and the country—

glimpses growing more and more tantalising as time went on, and as the movement of civilisation trod down the old beauties and delights of the Strand. The Strand, however, had magnificent compensation for its losses. It was like some rustic maiden who has been married by a prince: the rustic maiden wears no necklace of beads or chaplet of wild flowers any more, but she has a coronet on her head and a string of diamonds round her neck; she does not dance on the village green and under the maypole any longer, but she moves in the stately figures of the Court minuet. Which is the better part? That would have to be left to the village maiden to tell for herself, if haply she could tell it, which she probably could not. The Strand ceased to be the green shore of the Thames, and became the highway of kings and of history. Along that Strand either way moved the stately procession of England's imperial life; captive princes, captive kings, have passed along there; every English sovereign—I believe I may say every one: is there a single exception?—has passed in triumph along that favoured thoroughfare; the funeral processions of queens have gone one way, the funeral processions of heroes and conquerors have gone sometimes the one way and sometimes the other; even down to our own prosaic days the Strand has been allowed to keep up its character as an imperial highway. I can remember the funeral of the Duke of Wellington, that "most high and mighty prince," as he might well have been called—Marlborough was so called in the official records of his funeral pageantry. Men and women of only middle age can remember the wedding procession of the Prince and Princess of Wales, and the thanksgiving ceremonial when the fever-stricken Prince was given back to life. All this kind of moving splendour the Strand has seen; for this it has had to sacrifice its early countrified ways, its hedges, its flowers, and the river waves that melted on its banks.

Of late years, perhaps, it is a little falling

away in its august adornments. The processions of princes are becoming infrequent; we have no captive kings any more; and when a foreign sovereign comes here of his own goodwill and pleasure he does not always care to fare in public array along the Strand. No set of devoted Stuartists now make their way along the Strand, and, suddenly breaking out with appropriate emblems and devices on Ludgate Hill, vociferously proclaim the reign of James the Third. Even the Lord Mayor's Show begins to have less of a grip than it had upon the mind and the memory of the Strand—it only holds a sort of year-to-year lease of existence. It was, to be sure, revived and refurbished last year or the year before last, let us say, but who can tell whether the spirit of modernity—I have seen the word somewhere lately—or of economy, or we know not what, may not suspend its appearance for a year or two, and after that interval, supposing it to come, what may not happen? Has the Strand outlived its grand characteristic? "No longer steel-clad

Introduction 15

warriors ride along thy "—something or other —" shore." No, indeed, none such, except only the men in armour of the Lord Mayor's Show, and, alas! who believes in them? The more real, flesh-like, living they are, the more they are incredible and impossible; the more significantly do they proclaim that the Strand has no longer anything to do with the Middle Ages.

Well, perhaps the Strand is not altogether the worse for that—perhaps it is not wholly and merely a sufferer and a victim to the wrongdoing of time because it has lost the mail-clad warriors and even the processions of kings. I can well remember reading in one of the earlier volumes of State Trials the story of some murder committed at the setting on of this or that great disguised—I mean concealed—personage, some personage carefully kept in the background. The murder was not found out for many days, and why, does my reader think? Because the murdered body was hidden away "among the dunghills on the Strand at the end of Drury Lane."

Among the dunghills on the Strand a murdered corpse lying for days undiscovered! Are we not on the whole somewhat better off now? If we miss—supposing we ever do miss—the mail-clad warriors and the triumphant or captive kings, have we not the better of it, seeing that we are free of the murdered bodies stowed away amid the dunghills? Then the Mohocks—those awful gangs of "swell" rowdies who amused themselves by rolling women in casks down Ludgate Hill at midnight; and "tipping the lion," that is, flattening the nose, for peaceful and honest citizens returning home belated; and "pinking," and "sweating," and "tumbling," and all the rest of it—is it not something that we are free of these young "bloods" and their brutal practical jokes, and their torturing and witless buffoonery? I may say, perhaps, in order to be fair while I am dealing with this part of the history of London, that I believe there has been the most unreasonable exaggeration about the stories of the London Mohocks, just as there has been, perhaps, about the perils of the Thames Embankment in our own times. The Mohocks frightened Swift. He writes, in one of his letters to Stella, that people in London were afraid to stir out late at night because of them. The *Spectator* talks a good deal about them, and Gay, of course, has not left them unnoticed. Still, I cannot help believing, even from the very evidence of the period, that a few mad isolated pranks were exaggerated into a system of outrage, and that a brutal practical joke upon some wandering Paphian of Drury Lane was made to terrify respectable matrons and maids who were anxious to attend balls and parties late o' nights. If I am quite mistaken in this impression I should be only too glad that any one well acquainted with the London records and statistics of the time, such as they were, should point me to the trustworthy evidence which shows that the Mohocks were a really prolonged, and a systematic trouble to the London night-life of the time of Swift and Addison.

Even if, however, I should be right in my contention, that will not touch the point I strive to make when I insist that, on the whole, we who traverse the Strand have not lost utterly when we lost the mail-clad men and the processions of kings. Supposing, as I do suppose, that the doings and the dangers of the Mohocks were grossly exaggerated, what then? The panic was a distinct trouble; the scare was a very practical nuisance. We should not be much frightened just now if we heard of Mohock gangs east of Charing Cross of nights. We should go to the Lyceum Theatre, and the Gaiety, and the Adelphi, and Drury Lane, and Covent Garden, and all the other theatres, just the same; we should leave the police to look after us—and they would look after us—and the Mohocks, if they should present themselves, would be simply "run in," and would get ever so many days' imprisonment when brought up at Bow Street next morning. Does mediævalism mean picturesqueness, and modernity comfort? I do not venture to answer. And supposing it be so, which London — mediæval or modern — has the better part? "Alas!" as Hamlet says, "I know not."

II

CHARING CROSS

The Londoner as a rule never sees London. He never looks at it. He knows it all too well. He has grown used to it. He has given up looking at it and thinking about it. He may be very fond of it all the same. A man may be very fond of his daughter, but if on coming home alone some night he happens to see a light shining from the windows of her bedroom he does not stop beneath and contemplate the gleaming panes with eyes of reverential poetic love, as he used to contemplate the light in her mother's window long ago, before he was married. So with the Londoner and London. He may love the place, or, at all events, his own nook of it; he may be happy with his friends and his cronies and his favourite haunts, and his dinners and clubs and theatres and Parliament, and all the rest of it; but he goes along Pall Mall or the Strand and he sees nothing. The born Londoner is worst of all in that way. The resident Londoner who came to town from the provinces or from Ireland or Scotland remembers a time when he could not study London half enough for his own satisfaction, when every street had its own especial interest for him, and he looked at the houses as if he were inquiring into the riddle and the story of each of them. But he too subsides before long into the condition of the born Londoner, and he goes his daily way apathetic, and the Strand is a thoroughfare for him and Charing Cross is a crowded place where he has to dodge the omnibuses, and Strand and Charing Cross are nothing more to him. The monotony of his daily movement has made him blind to London, as the monotony of the snow makes men blind while they are mounting the Alpine steeps.

Happily there comes now and again a stranger with fresh, artistic eyes—an observer and a man of genius who re-creates London for us Londoners, and shows us what it really is—what it was to our own eyes while they could yet see it for themselves. Take, for example—a very remarkable example indeed—the drawings reproduced in this book, which are by the hand of a stranger. Mr. Pennell illustrates the street life of London from Charing Cross to St. Paul's. He reminds one of the familiar magician of the East who holds in his hand a little drop of ink, and somebody gazing steadily in sees there the realities of some scene and some life long unknown to him. Mr. Pennell takes his little drop of ink, and he dips his pen in it; and behold, in a moment we are all gazing into the street life of London. We are more than gazing into it; we are living in it—we are of it. These sketches were all evidently taken on the spot. How

FLOWER GIRLS AT CHARING CROSS

else should they be taken?—I can imagine some reader asking. Well, what I mean is that they were not taken by a man looking out of a window—say a man looking out of a window in Morley's Hotel, and sketching composedly the crowds far below him. Nor were they taken by a man seated comfortably in a carriage or a hansom cab stationary at the bottom of a street. Any one who will take the trouble to observe the sketches in the whole effect of each of them will see at once what I mean. These pictures come from the very middle of the crowd. A friend of mine made some capital Piccadilly sketches from a place of elevation on the roof of a cab; but the sketches had all the appearance of that quiet contemplation, that study from the upper boxes, which such a position would naturally give. The painter was drawing something which, if I may put it so, had nothing to do with him. He was drawing the street life of Piccadilly as he might sit on one of the terraces at Berne and sketch the outlines of the Oberland mountain-range.

But look at these Charing Cross sketches. Why, you feel as if you could see the artist running and plunging through the crowd. I think I can see him taking his stand composedly in one of the "refuges," and there steadily working away at his sketch until he has finished it, every figure and every house, and then plunging in among the omnibuses and cabs and crowd again, and shouldering his way until he gets another favourable place and makes another sketch. How he must have loved to do it all! How he must have revelled in it! How he has got the very atmosphere of each scene, the very life of each house! "The very houses seem asleep," says Wordsworth; and he was quite right, because he was looking at a scene of London in the early dawn. But in these sketches—sketches of the midday, most of them—the houses are all broad awake. Every group in the street, every single figure even, has a business and a story of its own. What would one not give for such a series of pictures of the life of that London which Dickens knew and made so real? That London is disappearing fast. There will soon have to be an edition of Dickens with copious explanatory notes on every page, or the younger readers will not know half the time what the author is talking about. Why, at this day a man or woman of twenty-one thinks of the Thames at Westminster as always bordered by a stately and somewhat monotonous embankment. What does he or she know about the rickety wharfs, the oozy old piers, the huge dark piles of warehouses, the tumbledown little old public-houses that once variegated the banks of the silent highway there? Even the elders forget all too soon how things were a few years ago. Only the other day I learned with much surprise—at first with a little or, indeed, not a little, incredulity—that the beadle of the Burlington Arcade is gone, that there has not been this long time back any beadle at the

Burlington Arcade. Can this be so, or was saucy youth merely playing pranks with me? Is he indeed gone, that stately, gorgeous creature who used to fill my young days with awe? Why, he was always there when I was a young man, and I pass through the Burlington Arcade a good deal still, but I never doubted that my old friend the beadle was always there. To say I never missed him would not explain the condition of things; of course, if I had missed him I should have found out all about him. I assumed him; I took him for granted; he was there for me, with a waistcoat which defied the hand of time and a cocked hat to which the gods had given immortal youth. And he is gone—has long been gone, they say. Who shall explain to the younger generation all about Northumberland House and the lion that used to surmount it— the lion that a credulous crowd was one day persuaded to believe it saw wagging its tail? Already Temple Bar is beginning to be forgotten; it will be disbelieved in by

TRAFALGAR SQUARE

the day after to-morrow or thereabouts. Soon a time will come when Londoners will take it for granted, if they think about the matter at all, that Addison may have sauntered along Shaftesbury Avenue, and that Sir Roger de Coverley may have put up at the Inns of Court Hotel.

That was a digression. I come back to Charing Cross and these sketches of streets and street life. They give a surprising impression of crowd and movement; a nervous, retiring person almost shudders as he looks on them; "I should not like to be hustling in that crowd," he thinks, "and dodging those cabs and omnibuses." In that masterpiece of farce-comedy—I do not know what else to call it—Ben Jonson's "Bartholomew Fair," the reader seems to feel the very dust of the fair getting into his eyes and his throat and making him thirsty. So in these sketches the confusion of the crowd makes a nervous man feel uncomfortable. He seems to be afraid to stand and quietly study them; he feels as if he could only get darting glimpses at them, as the artist himself must often have done. Some strange old picturesque front of a house strikes him much. Is there a house like that, he asks himself, a house like that so close to Charing Cross, where I thought everything was commonplace, and most things were new? He goes and tests the truth of the sketch by finding out the house. Yes, to be sure, there it is; there is the quaint, picturesque old-world front with the carvings over its windows. It is there, and I pass the place every day, and I never saw it before. Some day one of us will cross Trafalgar Square, and, suddenly looking up in a moment of awakened consciousness, will become possessed of the fact that the old National Gallery with its pepper-boxes is gone, and that some structure altogether different in style stands in its place. He will ask some benevolent passer-by about the matter, and will be told that the old building was taken down years ago.

CHARING CROSS

D

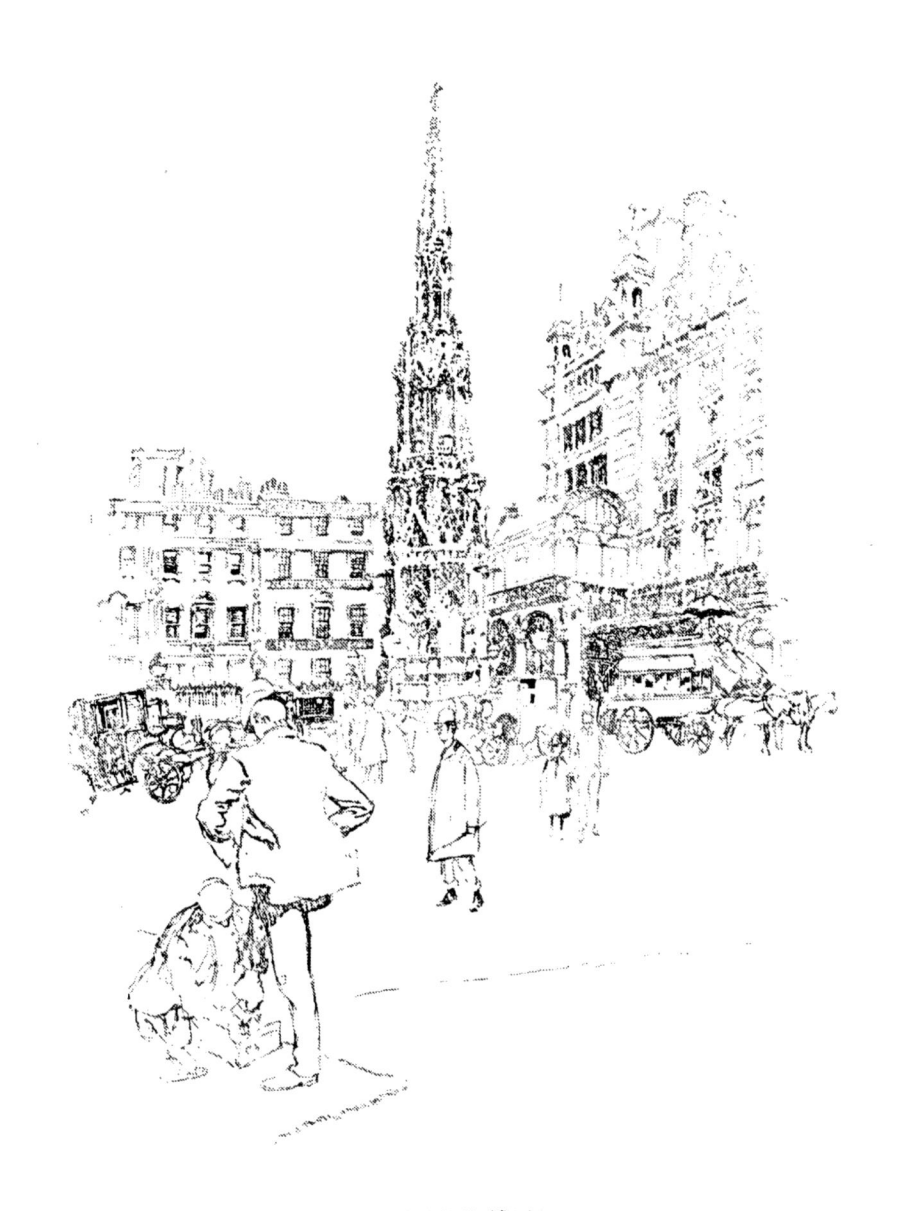

To a dreamy sort of personage like that —dreamy as a habit, but still interested in most things—these sketches of London ought to have an infinite charm. They give him the street life exactly as it is, but yet as he could not see it for himself; they give him the crowd without the discomfort of being actually in the crowd. If his dreams have a way of taking the form of stories and character studies, there are figures and groups enough here to feed him with material. Look at that young man who is standing to have his shoes blacked within sight of Eleanor's Cross. He is a well-made, well-set-up young man. He bends forward with eyes studiously turned downward. We cannot see his eyes, his back is turned to us; but we can know quite well from the bend of his head that he is looking carefully down. What is he contemplating?—the process of blacking his boots which is being carried on by the spry little lad, whose whole character can be read in the shape of his head and in so much of his nose as can be seen under the peak of his cap, his head being bowed over his work? No, I don't think the young man is wholly absorbed in the shoe-cleaning process; but I think his dress shows that he is from the country, and I don't fancy he likes being boot-blacked in the full sight of all Charing Cross, and so he looks down to hide his modesty. He is at the time of life when young men, especially from the country, really fancy that London is looking at them. I take this to be a very ingenuous, true-hearted young man. He is something in the engineering line, I fancy. I have a notion that he is staying at the Golden Cross hard by, and that he has just come out from the portals of that hotel, which must always have a tender interest for those who love David Copperfield. But I do not suppose that our young engineer went to the Golden Cross for the sake of David Copperfield—he is too young to care much about Dickens; but if he has not a sweetheart in London then I know

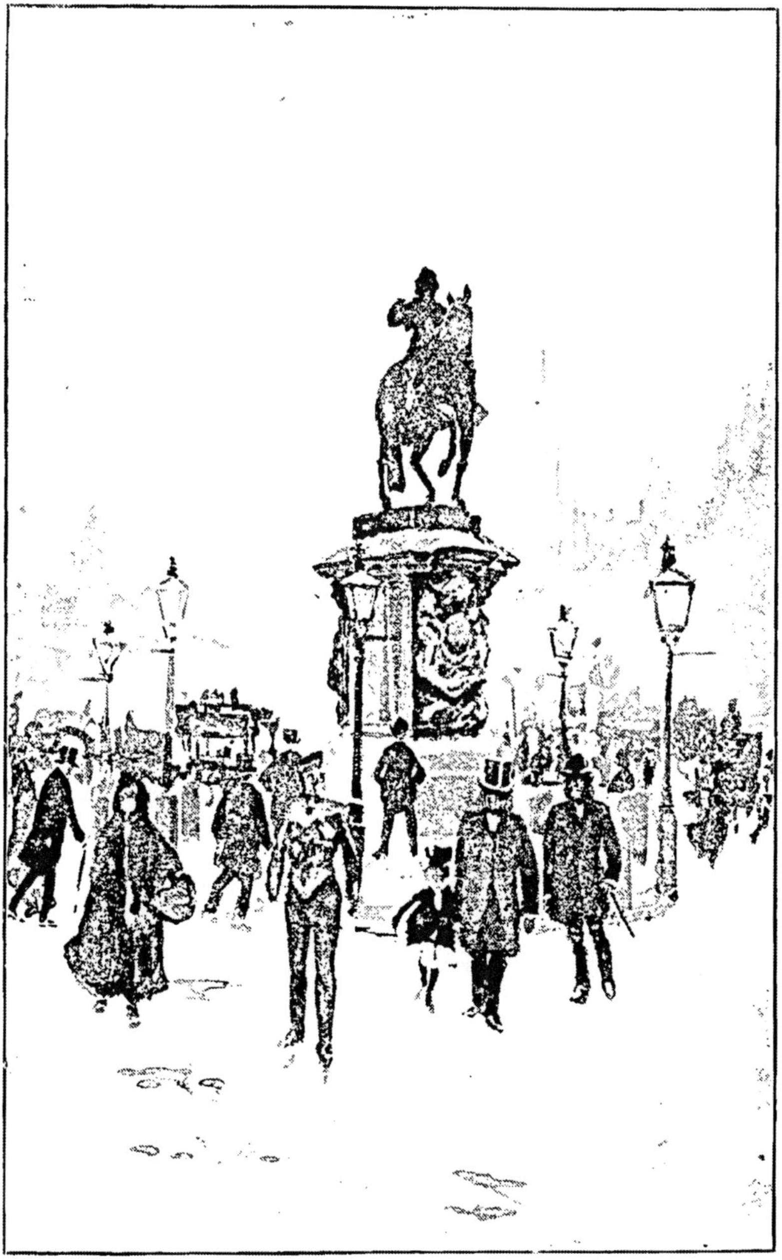

KING CHARLES'S STATUE

nothing of the world of fiction. Why, he is thinking at this very moment what an awful thing it would be if she were to drive by just then, and see him standing there with his trousers tucked up and having his boots blacked. But why did he have his boots blacked in the street? Why did he not have them looked to at the Golden Cross? He did—why, of course he did. But do you not see that the day is very muddy? Do you not observe the highly-tucked-up trousers of the careful man with the eyeglass who is picking his steps across the street? Our youth came out from the Golden Cross spick and span as regards his boots, but as he was hurrying along the street an omnibus bore down upon him and drove him into a puddle, and it would take too much time to go back to the hotel, and he just came on the boot-cleaning boy, and he is in haste to go and meet his sweetheart, who will be walking by accident in a Covent Garden flower arcade, and he certainly would not go to meet her in dirty boots; and so you see how it all occurs. He will go to the Lyceum to-night; he cannot see his sweetheart in the evening. Her people do not consider him quite up to her social level; but I am persuaded that he will get on, and will make a position for himself, and win the girl yet. You can see all this in his strong shoulders and his general air of self-reliance.

"Ah, bear in mind that garden was enchanted!"

These words are from Edgar Poe's charming verses, "To Helen." They explain how and why the poet came to understand all the phases of Helen's character, all the feelings of her heart, her "silently serene sea of pride," how boundless her ambition, yet "how fathomless her capacity for love." He only got a glimpse of her upturned face "and of her eyes upturned, alas! in sorrow" —one midnight in a garden, years ago. How did he come to learn all about her and to understand her in that moment's glance? He explains it thus—"Bear in mind that

MORLEY'S HOTEL, TRAFALGAR SQUARE

garden was enchanted!" So I say of the streets of London—in this particular instance, of Charing Cross. Bear in mind that the scene is enchanted. I shall go on this assumption all the time I am reading London street life through these sketches. That is how one comes to learn so easily the whole story of our young engineer, and even to know that he is an engineer. Can we not tell something of the story of that sedate and carefully-made-up man, in the drawing on page 37, who is crossing the street and holds a little child by the hand? He is a widower, clearly, and one who, I think, will never marry again. There is something of a set and square resolve about his prosaic, practical appearance which seems to tell of a man who will bear his loss bravely and not make futile attempt to repair it. How entirely different a picture is given by the other man, on page 33, who, with a little girl, is crossing the street somewhere near the young engineer! This man is jaunty, bright, very well dressed, very well satisfied with himself.

Either he is a young married man rather proud of walking out with his child and of being allowed to take care of her all alone, or the child is only a little sister of his—but this latter theory somehow does not quite satisfy me. No; I am sure he is a married man, and his wife is well and happy, but has not been able to come out with him, and he has taken the little girl to be his companion.

What different ways people have of crossing a street! Some men have such nerves that they can wind in and out among the cabs, and carts, and omnibuses, in imminent momentary danger which makes a mere looker-on tremble, and they never seem to think that they are in danger, but avoid every impingement and collision with the easy skill of a bull-fighter. See that man there—the wheel of a hansom has just brushed him and he steps ever so little aside and is unharmed. But the next moment he has come right in the way of a tearing omnibus, and the driver halloos to him and he coolly looks up and then allows just

ST. MARTIN'S IN THE FIELDS

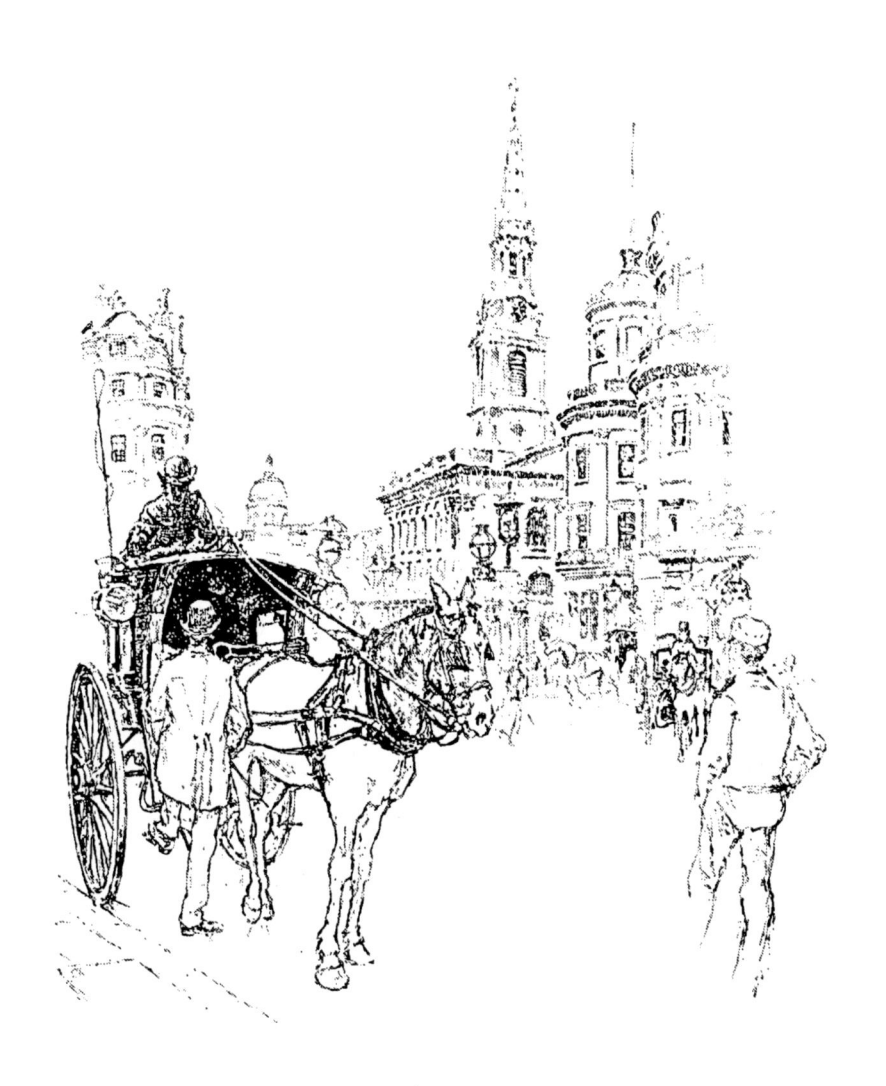

enough space for the omnibus to pass, while at the same time he contrives to keep his head barely clear of the huge planks that are being dragged on a great cart at his other side. The special danger of the London streets is in the variety of the wheeled traffic. You manage to get safely in front of an omnibus and quite clear of it, but you had not noticed the hansom cab which was coming rapidly along on the other side of the omnibus, and which now darts between you and the sidewalk for which you were making. While you are trying to dodge the cab, behold a mail-cart threatens you from one direction and a bicycle throbs its shrill flight and rattles its bell at you from another. The traffic up and down Broadway, New York, is probably greater than that of any part of London, but then it is nearly all heavy traffic—waggons and street cars and tramcars. There are few hansoms, few light carriages, and therefore few surprises for the pedestrian trying to cross from one side to the other.

To do our cab-drivers, especially the drivers of hansom cabs, justice, it must be said that they are wonderfully skilful and careful. If they drove with the recklessness of the Parisian drivers, London streets would be covered with the killed and wounded. Few sights inspire me more with curious admiration than to see a London *gamin*—perhaps a newsboy, perhaps a lad who gathers up street refuse—to see the joyous recklessness with which he disports himself among the wheels of the carriages and the hoofs of the horses. It is as if he could not be hurt by them, as if the danger that existed for others was no danger at all for him. He reminds me of the boy or girl of some far southern island disporting in the long sea-rollers flung in upon the beach. This southern island child is amphibious; has no more thought of danger from the waves than of danger from the pebbles on the beach; tumbles about as easily as if swimming in the sea and racing on the shore were just the same thing. So with the London street *gamin*. He is quite used to running in and running about amid the wheels and the hoofs, and he doesn't mind, bless you, and as I heard one of them say one day, " There ain't no harm going to happen to me." And I don't believe that any harm does happen to him in that way.

But look at some women crossing a street. I do not say that all women are bad at it. Some are composed, self-possessed, and majestic; they sail in and out among the cabs and omnibuses like stately yachts through a fleet of ironclads. Such a woman is now crossing near the Strand end of Morley's Hotel (see page 41); she holds a little girl by the hand and guides her; she moves slowly, steadily, hardly seeming to look either to the right or to the left, and yet with her calm eyes wide open to everything that concerns herself and her charge. Look at her—is she not a typical London figure? See how well she is dressed—with her fur-trimmed jacket tight over her firm, opulent bust, her skirts kilted exactly to the right height for a walk in London streets, her bonnet of the style next to the very newest —she would not think it quite right to have the very, very newest style of bonnet—her veil is drawn tightly across the upper part of her face and reaches just down to the tip of her nose; she is proper, prim, sensible, conscientious, innocent—probably never had a wrong thought in her life; her views, indeed, are limited—propriety is everything with her; she is the sort of woman who would not consider it by any means proper to wear very smart and lacey petticoats or other such garments; she has not two ideas in her head, and neither she nor anybody else would know what she could do with them if she had. Just now, however, I am watching her as she crosses the street, and I am full of admiration for her cool, successful composure. That is the woman who would not wince in a cold shower-bath when she had just pulled the string. I need not follow her in her passage—she will get across quite safely. But see how other women—the great majority of women—conduct themselves when they have to make a more or less perilous crossing. They begin with a sudden dart, then they think better of it, and come to a dead stand in the middle of the street just at the wrong time; then they try to run back again, and their affrighted gambolings sometimes stop the march of a streetful of traffic. I have seen women on the footpath of some perfectly quiet and little-frequented street pause a moment and take a long and anxious look up and down the thoroughfare, satisfy themselves that no vehicle of any kind is in sight either way, and then gather up their drapery in the most awkward and ungainly fashion and run as fast as their legs can carry them across to the other side, which they reach all panting and red with the air of shipwrecked people who have just managed to get on to a rock. I have seen women pause and look anxiously round and let the moment pass when there was a safe gap in the traffic, and then, just as the noisy waves begin to roll on again, suddenly make the dart at the wrong time, to the imminent peril of their lives. Worst of all is when there are two or three women together. They start off at the same time, but the moment they are in motion each seems to take a different view of the duties of the occasion. One thinks she had better rush on; another espies danger in that way, and quickly resolves to run back; a third comes to the conclusion that the best thing to do is to remain in the middle of the street. If each would be content to follow her own impulse and do nothing else it would not be quite so bad, but each wants to coerce her companions to do what she is doing, and there is a scene of pulling and pushing and arguing, and how any one of them ever comes alive out of that peril is more than I can understand. I do not want to put undue limitation on the rights of women, but I must say that I do not think a woman—at all events a modern and civilised woman—ever ought to run. Atalanta, of course—well and good—she was

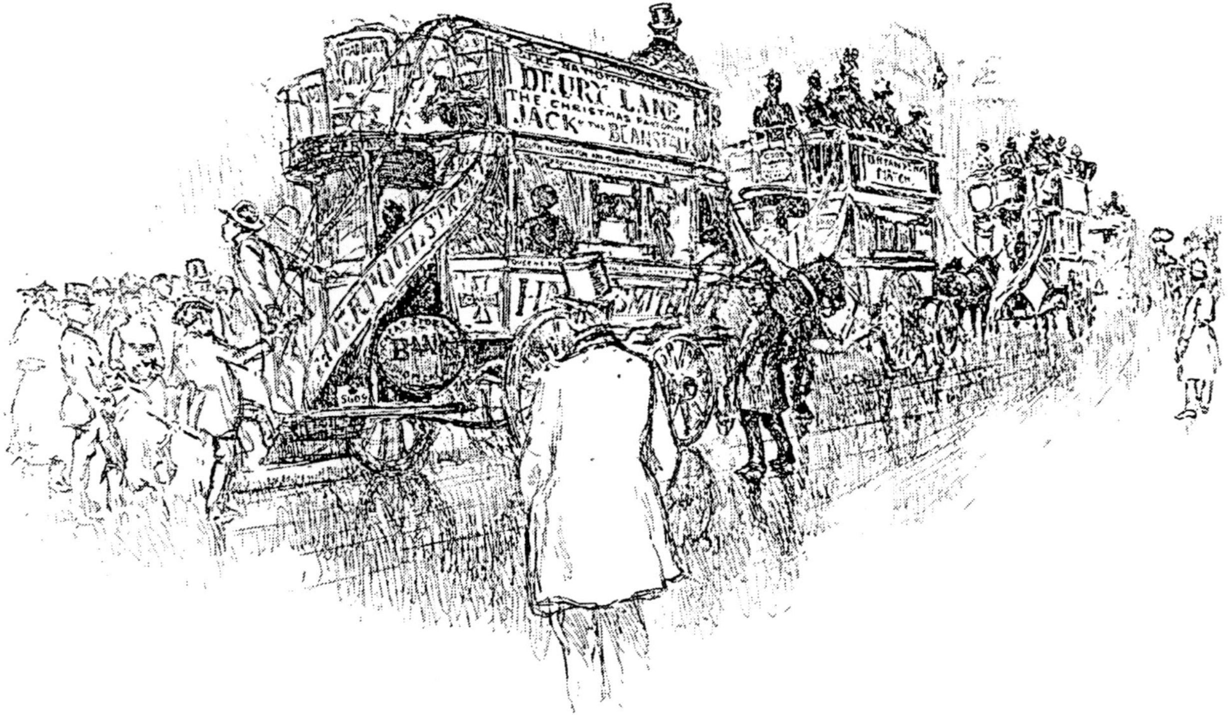
DRURY LANE
THE CHRISTMAS PANTOMIME
JACK & THE BEANSTALK

BUSSES

a sort of professional, and she got herself up for the task; she did not wear long skirts and high-heeled shoes and a bonnet with a little shrubbery or orchard or aviary on the top of it. Camilla, too, had a right to run— her tunic was short, and the grasses did not bend under her lightsome buskins—at least so the poet says, and poets ought to know —but the woman of modern civilisation and dress ought never to run.

We see a good deal of the soldier in these sketches. He is mostly a cavalryman, with his cap on the side of his head and his curious air of lounging alertness, not exactly swagger—there is too much self-complacency and self-content in him to call for the airs of a man who feels that he is bound to swagger. Can one wonder that the cavalryman is such a hero and idol to the servant-girl? Look at him, with his scarlet coat, his jingling spurs, his sabre, his moustache, his gold lace, his shiny buttons, his smart jacket, his tall, well-knit figure, and put yourself, if you can, in poor Mary

Jane's place, and think what a god of her idolatry he well may be! Think of the butcher's boy and the baker's boy who are her usual morning callers, and think how they would look beside that gorgeous soldier! Is there any corresponding womanly splendour which could equally dazzle the butcher's boy or the baker's boy? Does any woman ever come in his way as supremely dazzling and overawing as the cavalryman is to the maiden of the kitchen? Let us try to think. A ballet girl, perhaps, with her gauzy petticoats, and her pink legs, and her powdered and rouged face, and her smiles, and her suppleness, and her general splendour of attire? Well, no doubt she must seem to him like some creature from another sphere. And then the circus-riding woman in the velvet bodice and the short skirts and the pretty buskins, who stands upright on the horse's back and leaps through all the crashing hoops, and then at intervals drops down into the saddle again with pretty pantings of fatigue and bewitching little shudders of exhaustion; surely she must seem a vision of youth, beauty, and spangles—a plump phantom, if there could be such a thing, of delight? Yes, we may admit the ballet girl and the circus-riding girl; we may admit that they must in their radiance shine as dazzlingly on the butcher's boy and the baker's boy as even the cavalryman shines upon Mary Jane. But look at the difference. Where, I should like to know, is the ballet girl or the circus-riding woman who would condescend to go out for a walk with the young butcher or baker? He might as well expect Miss Ethel Newcome or Miss Mary Anderson to go out a-walking with him. So these divine creatures are divine indeed for him; they are stars that shine on him from a far sky, not lamps that burn to light his lowly way. But Mary Jane walks out with her cavalryman on the Sunday, leans upon his heroic arm, looks up lovingly into his eyes, sits beside him on the bench in one of the parks, is "a part of his life," as the heroines in the novels put it. Therefore,

Mary Jane's experience with her soldier lover is an experience that, to my mind, is quite unique. Aladdin with the princess was not in it, if a comparison had to be made. I begin to feel sorry for all poor young princesses. They could not by any human possibility find any mortal lover so delightfully above them in heroic splendour as Mary Jane has found in her cavalryman. Is she not on the Sunday the happiest of human beings?

Very likely she is, but I once caught a glimpse of a face at Charing Cross one hot day of last summer which expressed a greater concentration of happiness than I had ever seen on the human countenance before, or perhaps shall ever see there again. It was a hot day—glowingly, gloriously hot. Outside a public-house door stood the driver of a four-wheeler, his cab waiting for him. He held in one hand a pot of beer from which he had been taking a deep draught. He held the vessel sideways in his hand, and seeing that there was a good deal left he

FISH SHOP AT CHARING CROSS

stopped for a moment to think over the joy of the occasion and to take it in and become equal to it. There he was, happy in the past, in the present, in the near future. The pleasures of memory, the pleasures of hope, the pleasures of imagination! Think of that first deep, long draught! How delightful in the mere memory! That man would not abate one jot of the heat of that day lest in doing so he might lose any of the joy of the deep drink. But then, in this present interval of delight, and while he is allowing the witchery of the first draught to gladden his veins and his senses, comes the knowledge that there is a still deeper draught yet awaiting his good pleasure. So he pauses in his drink, slants the pot a little, looks down tenderly into its dark foam-curdled pool, and still thrilling with the joy of the past drink, anticipates the rapture of the drink that is soon to come. No, I never saw in life or in art any human face so beaming, so radiant with an all-ineffable delight, as the face of that cabman on that hot day at Charing Cross with his porter-pot in his hand. Have we got him in any of these sketches? No, not exactly. We have not got him; but we have got his cab. There it stands in the sketch of the street near the Eleanor's Cross. The cab, yes; but why not the cabman? Can you not guess? Why, of course, because the artist, like a true man of genius, recognised the fact that no mortal hand or earthly pencil could reproduce the expression of that measureless content—and the joy of the cabman's countenance, like the grief of Agamemnon's kingly face, was purposely evaded by art, and left unillustrated. Art bowed to each, sighed, and turned deliberately, nobly, resignedly away.

III

THE STRAND

I REGRET not being a man of fortune. I am sincere in the expression of that regret. I regret the fact because among other reasons I am denied the luxury of studying such streets as the Strand from the summit of an omnibus. A man whose time is his only money cannot afford so costly a joy. The top of the omnibus is the seat for the idle— for those to whom time is a thing to be killed like game, or for the hard-worked and poor, whose hours after work is done are, in the money sense, valueless. But a man like myself may not afford omnibuses. He must take the frequent hansom. If he goes about much he lives half his life in hansoms. He has to do it. It would not be satisfactory to save a few shillings by taking omnibuses, and as a reward for his economy have to put up with the loss of a few guineas. I have not been on the top of an omnibus for years and years, but I have many pleasant memories of long, delightful journeys thus made in days when all the world was younger, and seemed to me to be a good deal less in a hurry. I gaze with envy on the people who sit enthroned on the roof of the penny omnibus in Mr. Pennell's lively sketch. How characteristic are the faces of these people! See the rather pretty young woman with her veil drawn midway down her nose, and the foreign gentleman, with the moustache and the eyeglasses, and the self-assertive hat. And look at the elderly woman inside the 'bus. I should like to be on the top of that omnibus and to go whithersoever it went, and then to come back with it again. I used to love that sort of thing when I was a very young man studying London as a stranger —the only way in which London is really to be studied. It used to be a favourite way of mine to hail the first omnibus I saw and scramble on to the roof, which was a feat of gymnastics in those days—we had no spiral staircases to our omnibuses then—a feat no woman ever ventured to accomplish, or even attempt—and let it carry me whither it would. I well knew that it could not carry me to any region or any street which would not be full of interest for me. I should like to make some expeditions of that kind even now, and survey the streets and the crowds, and call up recollections of other such rides long ago, and revive reminiscences in every place.

I knew, long ago, of two brothers, young lads, in a seaport town in one of these islands, who in all their love of the river and the sea, and their boat and the broken waves, still yearned above all things to see London. London was to them simply the London of Shakespeare and of Dickens and Thackeray. They used to spend hours in picturing to themselves the delights of living in London.

They proposed to live in some pretty suburb, and to go to town every morning and return every evening on the top of an omnibus. This was their modest idea of life; they did not stop to think of any particular quarter of London as more desirable to live in than another; the point of the thing was the fact of their living in London, and in that sense being the owners of it—able to go about it and study it and be happy in it. It was a sort of London mania which was very contagious in those days among boys who had never been in London, and it got its chief impulse from Dickens. The elder of the boys came to London and settled there, and has been living there a great many years, and of course sees little or nothing of London now. The younger lad never saw London at all. He went out to the United States to make a fortune, with the express intention of returning to Europe and living in London. He never returned. The Civil War broke out, and although he never was wounded, yet in the damp night-watches and in the

IN THE STRAND

intrenchments the seeds were sown of the disease of which he died. And so he never saw London—never once. And I, passing through London this way and that, and wholly without noticing the streets and houses, suddenly happen to remember these old-time fancyings and aspirations, and to see him. There are a good many ghosts about the Strand that the Strand never sees. The longer one lives in London, the more the Strand comes to be a phantom-haunted thoroughfare.

Now, take the region which Mr. Pennell has chosen to picture in the sketch I have already mentioned—the sketch which brings in the penny omnibus. It is in the close neighbourhood of Somerset House. To me that part of the Strand is haunted by many ghosts—"the forms that men spy with the half-shut eye." Some memories of a vanished Bohemia of literature and art haunt me as I look on Mr. Pennell's sketch. Do I not remember a gifted, eccentric Bohemian who used to haunt a restaurant on the left side of the Strand as you go eastward to St. Paul's, and almost exactly opposite to the spot where Mr. Pennell's policeman checks the too reckless advance of one of Mr. Pennell's life-like, living hansom cabs? Do I not remember the account he used to give of his effort to find "a basis of operations" for the livelihood of the day? When he had twopence he was ready to start. He made for this particular restaurant, and he ordered a cup of coffee. One could get a cup of coffee for twopence in those days—can one now? I do not know; I do not drink coffee. There he had his basis of operations. He lingered over his coffee until some Bohemian friend lounged in, who, seeing him, invited him to have a drink. My hero declined, was pressed, declined again, and then compromised by saying he didn't mind accepting a veal-and-ham pie. So there he is started. With a veal-and-ham pie and a cup of coffee, a man who can digest such food is prepared to begin the world. Then, later on, another friend drops in, and our hero is now suffi-

THE STRAND

ciently fortified to accept a pint of half-and-half. Then he starts out in pursuit of work. He drops in upon editors and sub-editors, he pays a visit to publishers; perhaps he gets an order for some job of literary work—perhaps he even gets payment for some job already done—and then he goes to his rooms, or his room, wherever the location may be, and if he has work to do he does it, and if he has had a cheque he goes back with a light heart to the restaurant I have described and he orders a dinner, and if any of his friends be round, he stands a dinner bravely, and so pays off the frequent veal-and-ham pies and the pints of half-and-half, and he is started in the world once again. It will not matter if for another week he is impecunious, he will not be as Dr. Johnson subscribed himself, "Impransus"—he will not be in the condition of wanting a dinner. Only he must have his basis of operations to begin with—he has his code of honour like another. He will not go into that favourite haunt without the means of calling for something at once and of paying for it on the nail. With that to begin with he is safe. I think with a genuine pleasure that it was my happy chance on more than one occasion to advance the modest sum which enabled him fairly to enter the day's battle of life. He was a man of principle: he never sought to borrow more than was needed to lay down the basis of operations. He is dead long since. Earth lie light upon his grave—that is, if he cares whether it lies light or heavy. He made life lie more lightly than it otherwise might have done for many of us in those far-off days when the Strand was yet a wilderness of possibilities, a garden of romance, a battle-field from which one might come back a conquering hero, or on which one might, like my poor friend, "yield his broken sword to Fate the Conqueror." I do not suppose that sort of bitter struggle for life goes on now among the younger men who are fighting their way into London literature. I hope not. There are so many more newspapers and magazines of all kinds that fair employment ought to be got much more easily now than it was then. I am glad if all the old irregular days of literature are gone. I am entirely in favour of regularity and order; but it must be owned that the gipsy is artistically a much more interesting personage than the beadle, or even the policeman.

"Hallo, my fancy! whither wilt thou go?" I have been wandering away from Mr. Pennell's sketches of to-day's London into a London of I do not want to say how many years ago. Anyhow, it was a London when Thackeray, and Dickens, and Mark Lemon, and John Leech, and Shirley Brooks, and Leicester Buckingham, and Edward Whitty were still alive. But although one ought to keep to the Strand of the present, one cannot do it if he has any memories. The real and the unreal, the present and the past, get so mixed up that they cannot be kept asunder. Why, there is not a house, not a shop, we pass on our way eastward from Charing Cross to St. Paul's,

that has not a story and an association for
me—a story and an association connected
with some individuality of man or woman
to which I could put a name. Stop me
at any house you please on either side of
the Strand, and I shall have something to
tell you associated with that particular house
and none other. Perhaps I have never
crossed its threshold: what does that matter?
I met some one, saw some one pass, just
outside that shop; some great man, perhaps,
whose face I then looked on for the first
time, and do you think I could ever forget
that shop? See! from the windows of that
house near Exeter Hall I saw Kossuth go by
—saw that serene, majestic face, then one of
the handsomest faces one could look on—
saw him go by with the adoring crowd about
him. He was indeed the lion of a season
then—Kossuth then, Stanley the other day
—and in between how many and in what a
strange succession! The Emperor of the
French one day, and Garibaldi another,
and the Shah, and the Czar, and Buffalo

EVERY SUNDAY
STRAIGHT
TALK
YOUNG MEN
WR LANE
STRING BAND
PUBLIC SERV
NEXT SUNDAY
730
WR LANE
MUSIC

Bill! Not a spot along the whole length of the Strand but I associate it with some name and face of a passing celebrity. Just there, at the spot where Wellington Street touches the south side of the Strand, I saw Dickens for the last time. They have a saying in New York that if you take your stand on a certain part of Broadway, you will see everybody you want to see. The same thing might have been said, and much more aptly, of the Strand at one time. Perhaps it is not quite the same now. Westward the course of celebrity takes its way.

Exeter Hall! I have mentioned Exeter Hall, and here is the place itself as shown by Mr. Pennell. Exeter Hall is an institution; it has a history; its history ought to be written. I think the book would take —"The History of Exeter Hall." Forty years must have gone by since Macaulay roused a storm of anger against him by his famous allusion to "the bray of Exeter Hall." That was in the time when Exeter

Hall was associating itself mainly with movements against the Pope and the Jesuits, and against the political emancipation of the Jews. But Exeter Hall, apart from questions of creed altogether, has been the nursery of many a noble agitation in a good cause. The first time I ever heard Mr. Henry Ward Beecher speak was at a meeting in Exeter Hall. It was while the Civil War was going on in America, and he had come over to plead the cause of the North. The meeting was got up by the friends of the North, but the Southern cause was very popular in London society then, and there were numbers of the advocates of the South in the hall that night. Beecher's speech was rudely, and even savagely, interrupted in the beginning, but before long he made his opponents listen to him. I think Beecher was the most dexterous and powerful platform speaker I ever listened to, and that night he was put upon his mettle. His self-possession was superb; his good-humour unconquerable; his voice

TERRY'S THEATRE
2/6

TERRY'S THEATRE

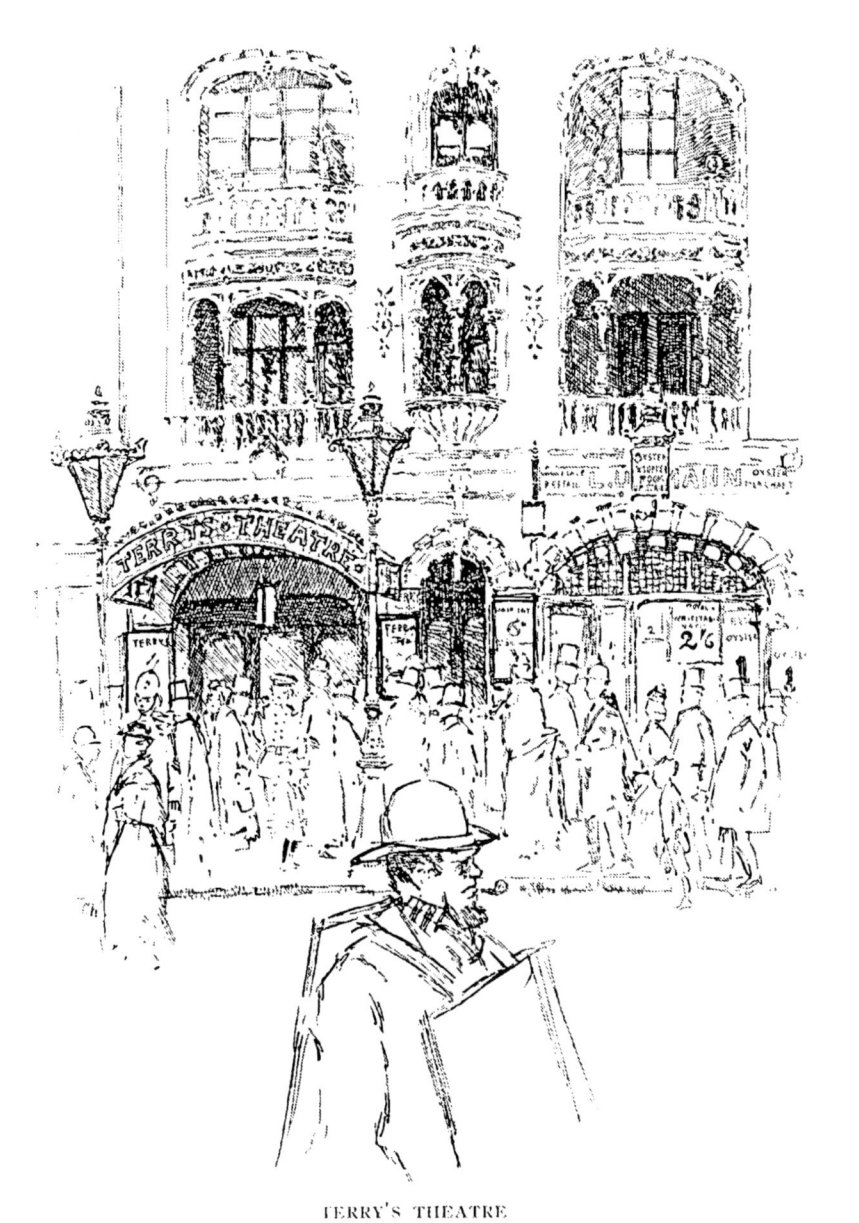

splendid; his readiness of reply was as the explosion following the spark. He was making some allusion to religion in the North, when some one sarcastically called out, "Religion and war!" meaning to imply thereby, no doubt, that religious nations do not carry on war. Beecher caught at the interruption. "Religion and war?" he exclaimed; "and what is the national emblem borne by the flag of England? Is it not the cross upon the field of blood?" At that time there was felt some dissatisfaction in England about an over-enthusiastic welcome given to certain Russian princes in the United States. We were then full of horror at the suppression of the Polish rebellion, and we hated the Russians. A voice called out during one of Beecher's thrilling sentences, "What about the Russians?" Beecher understood the meaning of the question, and he gave it a prompt reply. "I suppose," he said in a grave, deep tone, "you mean to condemn some of our great folks in my country because they seem to be coquetting with the Russians who enslave the Poles? You are grieved that they should do so. Well, so am I; and you will all the better understand how grieved we feel when your great folks coquette with the Southerners who enslave the negroes." The reply was all the more effective because it assumed the perfect good faith of the interruption, and admitted a sympathy with its purpose.

How well Mr. Pennell has rendered the austere aspect of Exeter Hall! No doubt he draws every scene exactly as he sees it and finds it—but if we did not know this we might be inclined to believe that he had exercised a little poetic fancy in making the very passers-by applicable in appearance to the character and the associations of the building. Observe the man with the strictly sleek hat and the shaven face and the eye-glass, looking indeed in some ways a good deal like a certain distinguished statesman and debater who has lately been occupying a very prominent and peculiar position. But this gentleman in the street picture, how entirely in harmony he is with the aspect of Exeter Hall! He is so primly well dressed, so very sedate and proper. And the cabmen, one this way, two that, drive slowly by as if they were passing a church during service-time. Contrast that scene with the look of the little crowd round the Gaiety, where, as we see, "Faust up to Date" was still going on. To be sure this latter crowd is a crowd attracted by " Faust up to Date" —it is a Gaiety crowd altogether. Where the Gaiety door is, there will the Johnnies and chappies be. But the Exeter Hall scene is a happy accident, for there does not seem to be any meeting going on just then inside, and the chance of street traffic enabled the artist to make the whole sketch a piece of harmony. It is worth while to notice the different appearance and manner of two men who are passing the door of the Gaiety, but do not belong to the crowd. They are much more in the foreground: of one we see only the head and shoulders. He is well dressed, but there is something distinctly provincial about him. He turns to look at the crowd with interest and sym-

THE GAIETY

pathy. He is not going in himself; he has some appointment which takes him elsewhere; but he would go in if he could. Yet he is not in any disappointed mood. I am sure he likes well to go where he is going, and does not envy those who have places in the Gaiety. Only he is a distinct sympathiser— he has been there before, and is sure to go again some night before he leaves town. But now look at the man with the soft felt hat, the close-cropped hair, and the moustache and beard. He goes grimly, morosely on, and never turns one glance on the frivolous little crowd round the Gaiety door. His mood is not in sympathy with such doings. He holds his mouth firmly shut; he looks straight before him in a dogged sort of way. Who is he, and what is the matter with him? Is he an artisan of the better class on strike? Is he a conspirator? Is he a man of naturally stern mood who hates amusement of all kind? I rather lean to the theory of the conspirator. He is one of some foreign fraternity, and something is in preparation about which he has no great hope, and he passes along the Strand brooding over it, and does not even know that there is a crowd of pleasure-seekers obstructing a part of the pavement. He moves along as unnoticed by them as his purpose is unknown to them. He and the young man from the country will pass each other closely in another second or two, but they have no more to do with each other than two ships that pass wide-parted on the ocean.

One could spin a little story out of almost every figure in these sketches—just as one could out of almost each separate figure in the actual life of the Strand. Because the artist has made each of his figures so full of life, so living, and where there is life there is story, as surely as where there is substance there also is shadow. But whether the life be the substance and the story the shadow, or the story the substance and the life only the poor shadow, I do not venture to say. It would carry one too far away to try to work out that problem. There is a figure, for instance, in the sketch which contains the omnibus—a figure ready-made for a story. It is the figure of a man who is crossing to the north side of the Strand, close to where

WELLINGTON STREET

the policeman checks the cab. There is a keen, cold March wind blowing; you can see that it is so by the manner in which the man keeps his hands deep set in his pockets, and by the shuddering outlines of his gaunt figure. He is very poorly dressed—those trousers and those boots speak eloquently, far too eloquently, the tale of "Hard-up." The whole sketch is only a few black touches, but we get the man complete and living, and we can easily find out his story. He has seen better days. He started in life well, but indolence first and misfortune after told against him, and he was never a man to fight stoutly against enemies, and if Fate stared hard into his face to stare sternly back at her—and so he succumbed and went down and down. Fate is very cowardly; she delights to inflict chastisement on those who readily submit to her; and on the ill-booted heels of this poor man "unmerciful disaster followed fast and followed faster." There was a girl once who loved him, shabby poor rascal as he looks now—she loved him and would have risked her happiness with him, but he had no ambition and he had no real courage, and she saw all this, and turned away disappointed—and she is happily married now, and only sometimes remembers the good-for-nothing lover of former days—the man with the old boots and with his hands in his pockets. See, even against the March wind he has not the courage to stand up stiff and defiant. He cowers and cringes before it as he cowered and cringed before other antagonists, and this is what he has come to. Let him pass; let us not follow him to his lonely home: no one could do any good for him ever again.

We get more than one impression of the Lyceum in these sketches. We see it by daylight, we see it by lamplight. The Lyceum, like Exeter Hall, is an institution, only of a different kind, and ought to have its history. My first recollection of the Lyceum goes back to the days of Charles Mathews and Madame Vestris. I was new to London then, and I had never seen such acting as that of Charles

THE LYCEUM

Mathews. I have seen a good many actors in a good many countries since that time, but I have never seen any one who could surpass Charles Mathews in light comedy. He holds in my recollection a place absolutely distinct, apart, entirely to himself. However, I am now discoursing not of Charles Mathews exclusively, but only of Charles Mathews as a figure in the history of the Lyceum. Then there comes a blank in my memory for some years, and Charles Mathews has ceased to be associated with the Lyceum, and all London that cares about acting at all is rushing to the Lyceum to see another Charles—Charles Fechter—act in "Ruy Blas." What a sensation that was! "Yesterday I was your servant; to-day I am your executioner!" How the pit rose at these words, and the magnificent gesture which gave effect to them! The Lyceum then fairly conquered Fashion. For at that time Fashion in London had given up going to what we call "the theatre," in the ordinary sense, and only professed to go to the Opera. But

Fechter, with his success, seized the heads of Fashion's horses, and turned the carriage round, and compelled it to land its master and mistress at the doors of the Lyceum Theatre. Then came "The Duke's Motto," which delighted Fashion even more than "Ruy Blas" had done. The unspeakably gallant and graceful bearing of the hero when he was playing his own part; the marvellous subtlety and craft when he was playing the part of the hunchback; the exquisite grace of Kate Terry, then in all the brightness and freshness of youth; the winning archness of Carlotta Leclercq, and the brilliant closing scene, "ringed with a flame of fair faces and splendid with swords," all this charmed the town with a new and delightful sensation. Then came the "Hamlet" over which there was so much controversy—the Hamlet of Delaroche, the Hamlet of Goethe, the Hamlet of the flaxen locks. That was the zenith of Fechter's fame; the rest was gradual descent. The last time I saw Fechter was at a dinner of the "Saturday Club" in

Boston, Massachusetts. Members of the club were allowed on certain days to introduce each a guest to the dinner; Fechter was the guest of Longfellow, I of Emerson. Wendell Holmes was there. But I am wandering away from the Lyceum.

Years go on, and there is another Hamlet in possession of the Lyceum, with another Miss Terry for the fair Ophelia; and Irving, too, has conquered Fashion, and made it a captive at the wheels of his chariot. For a while he disappears—is off to America to become the star of the New World theatres, and Mary Anderson makes her first appearance at the Lyceum, and bewitches her audience with Parthenia. She is timid at first, and speaks in a low tone. "A little louder, Mary!" a voice cries out from the back of the gallery; and Mary smiles at the well-meant familiarity of the interruption, and she speaks a little louder, and she has scored a new success for the Lyceum. Yet a little, and the Lyceum welcomes with all its acclamations the almost perfect Daly Company, with its superb actress and great artist, Miss Ada Rehan, and we all acknowledge with ready rapture that "this is the Shrew whom Shakespeare drew." Yes, the Lyceum has a splendid record in the history of the stage. It has been a sort of academy of dramatic art. Its pupils and students go out and teach the world.

The picture-shops and the photographers' used to be the delight of my early days, and indeed I stop every now and then even still to *afficher* myself to some winning window. There is one shop—should I call it a shop?—is not that word far too lowly in its import for the establishment I speak of?—with which I have certain tender associations. Some seventeen or eighteen years ago I was looking in at its windows one day, and a story about it came into my mind. I had long been in the habit of studying its windows. It stands at the corner of one of the streets running off the Strand—but not for worlds would I make known the name of the street at the corner of which it stands—and it exhibits rich store of pictures, statues, statuettes, and curi-

BURLEIGH STREET, STRAND

osities—silver, gold, bronze, and all sorts of delightful things. I never was near the place but I went to the windows and studied them. And I got into my mind—it came on me quite suddenly one day—a story about it. How if it should happen to be owned by a man—I do not know to this day who owns it—who had two pretty daughters, and whose highest ambition in life was to have them, or one of them, married into rank? He had the repute of having plenty of money, and indeed lent, in a private and confidential and perfectly honourable way, money on the fairest terms to embarrassed gentlemen who were known to him as clients. And everything goes wrong for a while, and everything comes right in the end—and I shall not tell my story all over again: this is not an advertisement. Only I am inclined to point out the curious relationship in which a certain house may stand to a writer of fiction—a house which, he knows not how, has inspired him with a subject. In that house are dwelling for him beings whom the owner of the house has never met and knows nothing of. I never pass that house but I see my heroine and her shadowy kith and kin, and her lover —and all the rest of them—and the owner of the house, I daresay, never heard of my heroine—and for that matter never heard of me—and I know nothing about him or his family. I only know that I have installed there for myself another family whose names do not appear upon any rate-books, and no member of which ever records a vote at the parliamentary elections for the Strand Division of London. There is another street running off the Strand in the same neighbourhood, a street also running to the river, in which is a house wherein lived one of the heroes of my fiction. There is a set of tiny chambers in Agar Street, off the Strand, about which I dreamed a melancholy little story. It is hard for a somewhat dreamy personage like myself to take the Strand quite seriously. One has made it so unreal—one has hashed up in such inextricable confusion the real and the unreal. The scent that comes from Rimmel's shop brings back all youth to me. Why? Simply because I used to look into Rimmel's windows and inhale their scents when I was a very young man. Nothing carries with it a richer association than the breath of some scent. It is like magic. Music itself—which *is* magic—can hardly equal it. You are wandering along the streets thinking of nothing—along the Strand—you are moving through just such a crowd as our artist sets living before us—and you are utterly commonplace. And suddenly some breath of perfume is borne in upon you—from a flower-girl's roses, or even from the made-up contents of Rimmel's window-cases—and behold! one is living all at once in another and an enchanted world —the world one lived in or fancied he was living in years and years ago. Once, not long since, I was passing down the Strand, and there were some repairs going on—and I caught the odour of a pitch-kettle—and in a moment I was back to the seaport home of my boyhood again, and to the sound of the breaking waves.

IV

THE STRAND (*continued*)

THERE are a few delightful old houses still to be seen at rare intervals on either side of the Strand. They are the old houses with the overshot windows, which suggest the days of Chaucer. Some of them may be seen in Mr. Pennell's sketch of the little crowds looking in at the windows in the near neighbourhood of the Strand Theatre. These sacred old-time houses are fast disappearing. Soon they will have gone altogether. Every lover of poetry and history and art, of whatever kind, ought to be sorry when these houses and their memories are gone. I find no fault with the spick-and-span new redbrick houses, ever so much more Queen-

THE STRAND, BY SOMERSET HOUSE

Anne-like than the houses of Queen Anne's own day. Many of these new houses are very beautiful buildings, and where there are whole streets of them the streets are, happily, not allowed to be monotonous. The architects who delighted in such creations as the Quadrant in Regent Street are not in practice now. I should not feel much regret if the revival of Queen Anne architecture were to mean the pulling down and obliterating all remains of the hideous Georgian houses, with their formal, commonplace monotony. But one must lament for the few really old houses—for the fewer still that are left of the dear, delightful old hostelries. Is there no way of preserving even a few of these old buildings, in order that a future generation may be able quite to understand what Chaucer is talking about sometimes? Could they not be kept up as national monuments? I often wonder that somebody in the United States does not offer to buy some of them, and take them over—stone by stone, brick by brick, rafter by rafter—and set them up again, all standing, in Central Park, New York, or on Boston Common. I wish some American would make the offer and transplant the houses. For over there they would be admired and preserved, but if left to us they are sure to vanish. You can see them better in Mr. Pennell's sketch than you can in the street. In the sketch you can study them at your leisure, and as long as you like; in the Strand you are hustled along by the crowd, and you can only get a good look at them even for the moment by crossing to the other side of the street. How oddly they contrast with the new houses, some of which are their near neighbours—with the red bricks and the tiles, and the prison-bar-like windows, and the doors set deep in cells, and all the other old-new ornamentations of architecture! What will some future generation think of this general revival of the age of Queen Anne—this deliberate architectural masquerade and fancy-dress exposition? Goethe somewhere said it was well enough to wear fancy dress and become a Turk or a

Venetian senator for part of a night, but he could not understand being a sham Turk or Venetian senator for one's whole long lifetime. Yet there are people, undoubtedly, who do go through their whole lives thus masquerading—putting on the airs of something they are not, and never were, and never can be. Are we not doing something of the same kind with our streets and our houses? But the more we carry on this architectural *renaissance*, the more fondly do I wish we could preserve such of our ancient houses as are still upreared among us. Let us, if possible, have some of the real old time to console us for the unreality of the sham old time. London was real once. Why allow every evidence of the reality to be effaced?

Then there comes another thought. Queen Anne revived will, of course, only have her day. Even a ghost cannot live for ever. Men will grow tired of the red-brick houses and the Queen Anneism. They will want something else. In some far-off generation is it not possible that a fancy might come up for the revival of Queen Victorianism in street architecture? All very well, but what will there be to revive? The age of Queen Victoria has not any architecture of its own. It inherited the hideous remains of the Georgian times, and it came in for the restoration of Queen Anne. If the latter movement goes on much further it will soon have obliterated every trace of the London which Queen Victoria looked on when she went forth to her coronation, or paid her first visit to the House of Lords. To be sure there is what may perhaps be described as the Pimlico order of architecture—the stucco-faced house with its ridiculous attempt at a Greek porch, which house, multiplied by many and divided into two lines, constitutes a Pimlico or "South Belgravia" street. Nothing else in the way of street building ever was half so hideous. The worst of the Georgian streets is like Venice, or Nuremberg, or Oxford, by comparison. It gives one a sinking of the heart to look down the ruthless

SOMERSET HOUSE

monotony of a Pimlico street, with every house exactly the same size and shape as every other, and not a tree to refresh the saddened, sickened eyes. But let us hope that revived Queen Anne may be remorseless, and, like the jaws of darkness, devour up these dreadful structures, and leave it to be said in history that in Queen Victoria's age men did not build; they only revived.

In the meantime we are in the Strand, and not in Pimlico—for which give praise. The sight of one of the windows in these Chaucerian houses revives the spirits. The prettiest associations curl, and twine, and play about it, like ivy or like smoke. One can see some winsome girl peep out of that window to look at her lover riding by, as he goes westward to attend the King. The King, of course, is Edward the Third. Why should not the lover be Chaucer himself, in the days of his early courtiership, and his early courtship? Why should not the girl looking out from the window be Philippa herself—the Philippa whom he afterwards married—in the days before he went soldiering and was taken captive, and got home again, and was made Comptroller of the Customs at the port of London? Yes, Philippa it is, Philippa it shall be, who looks down from her overshot lattice window and sees her courtly, gallant lover ride by; and he waves his plumed cap to her, and makes his horse caracole just a little to show what he can do in the way of horsemanship, to make her start first and smile afterwards. Somerset House, as we go along, dispels the poetic illusions—for even Old Somerset House, if we could see it, would be far too modern for any association with Chaucerian times, and the Somerset House we look on is a thing of the day before yesterday.

Look at the ragged woman selling, or trying to sell, her newspapers containing the "result of the Grand National." There are face and figure to bid the poetic begone and the hard, grim realistic take its place. There is the nineteenth-century struggle for life brought down to its meanest, its saddest. Mr. Pennell has done well to fix that figure on the mind and memory. England's national prestige, the glory of the empire on which the sun never sets—yes, it is splendid to think of that greatness and that glory—but just look there, look at that old woman! How many hundreds of thousands of her, how many millions of her, I wonder, are there in these two islands? Some day we shall have to put the big politics, the grand politics, the grandiose politics aside for a little, and take account of *her*. Now let us buy her paper; that is about all one can do for her. I do not myself know what the Grand National is, but let us buy a paper for the sake of that poor, ragged old woman, who is certainly national enough in her way, but about whom there is not much of grandeur anyhow. The sun which never sets on imperial glory has set long since on this poor old daughter of England. Somehow, I don't know how, I cannot think but that her condition dims the lustre of imperial glory. I always feel greatly interested in these street figures, as one might call them—these inhabitants of the streets, these poor things, young and old, who make a living in the streets—to whom the pavement of the Strand is their Stock Exchange, their mart, their Royal Academy Exhibition, their court of law, the stage of their theatre—the flower-girls, the boys who scrape up refuse, the men who sell cheap toys, the men who have stands for the sale of photographs. Now the inventions of science promise by degrees to knock away all their chances of making a living, such as it is, out of the passing crowds on the Strand. We shall stand before a machine, we shall drop a penny and take our chance of a photograph—it may be Cardinal Manning or it may be Miss Nellie Farren; or when some public personage is monopolising attention it may be that he will have a machine all to himself, and that we shall drop in our penny and take out our photograph of Mr. Stanley. All the same the wandering photograph-seller who lives up and down the Strand will find his poor little business taken clean out of his hands. No doubt we shall have some invention for the sale of flowers in the same way, and the cheap toys will be sold off by process of machinery, and there will be a company started for the mechanical collection of street refuse, and even the sellers of the evening editions of the newspapers will find their occupation gone from them. I have often wondered, by the way, why London does not have any street stalls for the sale of newspapers and magazines and cheap books, as the great American cities have. You never need want for a newspaper in a great American city. You have only to keep on a little and you will soon come to a goodly stall on the side-walk, covered up with newspapers, and magazines, and cheap books—just, in fact, what you only see at a railway station here. I know what a business it is to get a particular newspaper if you are in the House of Commons and the House does not happen to take that particular newspaper in. You would have to send miles to the newspaper office. I have sometimes crossed to the Westminster Bridge railway station and asked for permission to go on to the platform and hunt up the paper there. But if our Parliamentary buildings were managed after the fashion of Washington, one would only have to pass out into Westminster Hall to find a capacious bookstall, loaded with all the journalistic and literary delicacies of the season. I do not, somehow, see the great superiority of our system. But in truth we are only beginning to be a newspaper-reading people. We are even yet ever so far behind the people of the United States and the Canadians in that way, and even the people of New York do not, I think, come near the people of tiny little Athens in the passion for the devouring of newspapers. Why, the Square of the Constitution after the *cafés* have closed looks as if it were covered with snow, owing to the mass of papers lying about that men have read and thrown away. The Viennese, too, are a newspaper-reading population, and so of course are the Parisians. But the Parisians do not touch upon the New Yorkers, nor the New Yorkers upon the Athenians. We Londoners are

ST. MARY-LE-STRAND

pretty low down so far. For inventive energy I think, however, our newspaper-selling boys and men might hold their own against most of their brothers in the trade. The New York newsboy is an astounding little fellow, with his indomitable energy, and his unwearying good spirits, and his quenchless eagerness for trade; but I do not think he allows himself to invent much. I remember being stopped once in a cab, as I was driving home from a theatre on the Strand, by a boy selling newspapers, who implored me to buy the latest edition, containing the full account of the shooting of Mr. Parnell that evening by Mr. Charles Bradlaugh. I did not purchase, and the event was not recorded in the morning journals of the following day.

Near the old houses in the Strand Mr Pennell has given us a characteristic figure. It is that of a man with a great bloated face, and a pipe in his mouth. Probably it is only the human countenance that could be so completely divorced from all shade of expression No doubt the man is enjoying his pipe, but his face betrays no gleam of delight which might give us the satisfaction of knowing that a human creature is happy. He seems to be of the costermonger class, and the costermonger, I should fancy, contrives to get a good deal of a rough practical sort of enjoyment out of life. But this man is all stolidity. He sucks his pipe and pushes his way, and seems to have no concern with emotion of any kind. This is a face one sees very often in London. One does not see it so often, or often at all, in the great provincial cities, such as Manchester, Liverpool, and Glasgow—one does not see it at all, I think, in Paris or in New York. In Paris one sees many faces sullen, scowling, and discontented—men with old and new revolutions gleaming in their fierce eyes. But the face of actual and complete stolidity is to be found in its best specimens in London. I wonder whether that man with the pipe ever thinks of anything? When he goes home at night after his day's work does he ever review life at all, and take into account how much it is worth to him? Or does the pipe supply the place of all the futile thought and hopeless self-scrutiny wherewith most others of us mortals are wont to perplex ourselves by way of recreation? Would that man do a noble action if it came in his way to do it, or would he, under like conditions, commit a crime? I am almost inclined to think that he could not do a noble action or commit a crime, because nothing would be a noble action or a crime to him. The thing would not present itself to him in that light. If he did a good deed it would not be because he thought it good, or thought about it at all; if he committed a crime it would only be as the machine at the railway station gives out its packet of butterscotch or its cigarette. I do not think the study of that face makes one quite exultant about the blessings of civilisation in London. It must be curious—if one could get to the inside of it—the life of a man who never reflects. We know what an inferior and good-for-nothing creature is the man who never to himself has said that this, whatever it might be, is his own, his native land. But this man with the pipe probably never said anything to himself about his native land—it probably never came into his mind that he had a native land, and he would not have troubled himself to care about the fact even if he recognised its existence. Has he even a vague dislike somehow and somewhere to the French or the Russians—or the Irish, maybe?—I hardly think so. I can hardly believe he has reasoned himself far enough to get up any such emotion. I have sometimes been amused, when having to wander about obscure parts of London, to find how many people there are who do not know the name of the street in which they themselves are living. They have hired their poor little lodging, and perhaps have occupied the same lodging for a long time—in many trades and quarters the populations are not at all nomad—and they know where their home is, and can find it every night

ST. MARY-LE-STRAND FROM THE EAST

without a mistake; and what more should they want to know about it? What does it matter to them by what name somebody has chosen to call the street? It is their street—the street in which they live—and that is enough and to spare for them. I am inclined to believe that this man with the pipe never asked himself or any one else the name of the street in which he lives.

Near Somerset House a man is crossing the Strand. He wears a double eye-glass, through which he is peering as he crosses, apparently looking for some name or number on a shop. He has a full beard and moustache, and a handsome, well-moulded face. He has left middle age a little behind—he is making towards sixty—but there is a freshness, there is an elasticity about him which still carries with it a perfume and a savour as of youth. I think he takes life now pretty much as he finds it. He has thought out most questions as far as he could, and then at last come to the conclusion that it would be better to let them think themselves out without any trouble on his part. He belongs to one of the artistic professions, I am sure. I should be inclined to set him down as a genial literary or dramatic critic. He has written books and plays in his time, and they were good in their way, and had a certain sort of success; but they were not good enough for *him*. He recognised the fact that he had not the sacred fire of genius in him, and he did not care for mere respectability in literature or the drama. So he gave up creative work of any kind, and took to journalism—to criticism, and what are called "society leaders," and, indeed, leaders on all manner of light and bright subjects. He is really an admirable critic, because he is intensely sympathetic. He approaches every book or play he criticises with a sincere desire to find something good in it. If he really cannot say anything good of it he would much rather say nothing at all about it. But when, as in the case of a play, for example, he cannot let it pass unnoticed, then he gives his

OLD HOUSES IN HOLYWELL STREET

opinion, gently indeed, but very firmly; and those who know him, and who have not seen the play, put the criticism down when they have read it with the firm conviction that that play will not hold the stage for long. Pretensions of any kind make him angry, and he hates to be sought out and done homage to by certain authors and actors who only court him because they want to get him to notice them and to praise them. He lives mainly in the Garrick Club, and he is a great favourite there, as indeed he is wherever he is known. He is fond of talking about Thackeray, whom he knew, and it may be that some of the younger members of the Club think he talks a little too much about Thackeray, whom they did not know. There is a story about his having been much in love in his early—indeed, not very early—days with a woman who first was of opinion that she loved him, and then became of the opinion that she loved somebody else, and married that somebody accordingly. She was not happy with the somebody, and the somebody died, after having led her a hard life for many years. Then most people thought our friend the critic would marry her, but he did not. Perhaps he thought he could not trust his "fause true-love" any more. Perhaps he had settled down to his own free and comfortable bachelor life. Perhaps he had grown out of all poetry and sentiment: but that does not seem likely. Anyhow, there he is, going off to the Garrick very likely, and he will dine there, and go from there and look in upon a theatre or two. Later he will get back to the Garrick, and will meet Mr. Irving there, and Mr. Bancroft, and Mr. Beerbohm Tree, and Mr. Harry Furniss, and that most polished of orators and brightest of wits, Mr. David Plunket, and "Joe" Knight and Comyns Carr, and ever so many more delightful companions.

I have spoken of anecdotes about Thackeray, and acknowledged the fact that younger men sometimes think the subject wellnigh exhausted. Still, with that knowledge full in my mind, let me tell a little anecdote of my own about Thackeray and the Garrick Club. Many years ago I was invited to dine at the Garrick by a man well known about town in those days. He was a man of some means, and "by way of being" a literary man, and he had the reputation of being somewhat of a snob in Thackeray's sense of the word. That evening he began talking to me about Thackeray, and saying, as many people were fond of saying at the time, that Thackeray was a more complete snob than anybody pictured in his own book. I knew little of Thackeray personally, but I did not believe then, and I do not believe now, the accusation of snobbery made against him. So I disputed my friend's assertion. Whereupon he proceeded to give me evidence. "Why, in this very room," he said, "Thackeray came to me yesterday and offered me a cigar, and accompanied his offer with the words, '*You* ought to think highly of that cigar, for it was given me by a noble marquis.'" Yes, the story is perfectly true, and my friend did not see in the least that

Thackeray was chaffing him; was perhaps a little too open in his allusion to my friend's supposed personal weakness—his too tender devotion to the aristocracy of Great Britain. My friend never knew, I venture to think, why I smiled so much at his interesting anecdote. There, I have told my Thackeray story, and do not intend to tell any other. "We don't talk of Nathaniel Hawthorne any more," a literary man said to me not very long ago in Boston. New men come up and must have their turn. "Marry and amen," as Browning would say. By the way, the motto of some popular edition of Browning might well be found in the passage to which these words belong. They are, if I remember rightly, in the prelude to *The Ring and the Book*. The poet has addressed the British public, "Ye who love me not," and then a little later on come the words, "Oh, British public, who may love me yet—marry and amen!" The time has arrived; the British public does love him at last.

In my early London days there used to

ST. CLEMENT DANES

be talk of a haunted house in—where does the reader think?—why, in Norfolk Street, Strand. What an idea! A ghost in that prosaic region of the absolutely commonplace! Yes, the ghost was talked about, and it was said to be attached to a lodging-house, which was falling into decay accordingly. There was no Psychical Society in those days, and no scientific and organised attempt was made to find out all about the ghost, though I think some amateur efforts were made in that direction with the consent of the proprietor of the establishment. Nothing appears to have come of them, and the story died away. May it not have been, however, that if there ever was a ghost in the house it was a ghost personally conducted thither by one of the lodgers? Men of decayed family, when summoned to town on business, often put up in one of those Norfolk Street lodging-houses. As everybody knows, there are family ghosts attached to certain ancient houses, particularly Scottish and Irish houses—ghosts of a nature like that of the dog who goes about with his master, as well as ghosts of the nature of the cat who abides by the family hearth. Why may not some ghost of the former order have come up to London with the head of the family and stayed in Norfolk Street, and wandering inconsiderately about the passages at midnight have scared some belated lodger, and so set wild rumour afloat? Then, of course, when the head of the family called for his bill, and had his trunks packed and went away home, the attendant spectre would go away home with him. I wonder what would happen if two travellers brought two ghosts with them? Or suppose into some house already haunted by its own ghost there were to come a visitor with his family apparition in his train? Would there be a fight, as Artemus Ward puts it in reference to his probable meeting in the happy hunting-grounds above with the red-skinned brother who had robbed him down here on earth? Do ghosts speak to each other when they meet? Do they feel in this strange material world as two Englishmen might do who met in China, and assume that no ceremony of introduction is needed between two kinsmen of race meeting in such an out-of-the-way and foreign region?

We are getting to the region of the Law Courts. Positively I have to stop and pull myself up, and think what that part of the Strand was like before the Law Courts were begun. Temple Bar, of course, one recollects; and there was a queer little shop kept by a barber and hairdresser, and there was a passage, a sort of *cul-de-sac*, opening out of the Strand somewhere about the spot where the principal entrance to the Law Courts is erected—and I think it was called Pickett's Place—and I remember a sad story connected with it. Sad; yes, to be sure, but very commonplace in its catastrophe, although not perhaps in all its progress. It is only the story of a young man in somewhat delicate health who came up to push his way into London literature. He had great gifts and he had a good start. He began to write for some of the best of the magazines and for a daily newspaper. But he turned one day into this dull little Pickett's Place, and there he found his fatality. Fate came to him in the shape of a pretty, coquettish woman who kept a cigar shop. He fell in love with her. She was a married woman, but her husband had left her. My young literary friend fell madly in love with her. It was more like a case of sheer insanity than any other love-madness I have ever known. I have sometimes thought of describing it in a novel, but it would not do. Nobody would believe it. That is the worst about the events of real life: you cannot always venture to make use of them in fiction, for the reader will say they are too improbable to be even interesting. It was not merely that my friend gave up his whole heart to her—that anybody might have done for a woman—but he gave up his whole time to her. He spent his every day in the little shop in Pickett's Place. He dropped his club, he was never seen at his once familiar haunts. He took her out to dinner at some quiet tavern every evening. The whole day long he sat in that shop talking to her. He neglected his work, gave up his engagement on the daily paper; did nothing but hang after the skirts of this pretty, saucy young woman. I often used to wonder how he did not feel ashamed of being seen all day long in that cigar shop by every one who chose to go in. His friends soon came to know that if they wanted to see him they must go to the shop in Pickett's Place. He ceased to write to his people at home; when they wanted to know anything about him they wrote to me, and I softened things as well as I could. At last I recommended that the young man's mother should come to town and talk to him. She did come, and they had some sad scenes. Nothing could be done. He told his mother that he could not live without this woman's love, and that he meant to hold on to her in the hope that her husband might drink himself to death, and in that event he was determined to marry her.

He told his mother that there was nothing wrong between them, which I firmly believe, for the little cigar-woman was determined to marry him, and I felt no doubt that she would maintain a rigid propriety in their relationship. I went to her once as a private ambassador from the family, to ask her whether she was not prepared to take what Mr. Labouchere once called "a financial view of the matter." She laughed at the proposition. She was not prepared to take a financial view—*that* financial view—of the matter. She was determined to marry the young man, and then everything would be hers, she said. So I dropped out of the business, and only saw my infatuated friend from time to time. He gave up his whole life to this woman—his life, his family, his prospects, his literary career, his intellect, his education, his mind, his heart, his better nature, his very soul, to this brainless and unfeeling little creature. At last the husband did "dree his weird," did drink himself to death, and my Antony was married to his Pickett's Place Cleopatra.

Then the wife's one grand calculation proved a complete miscalculation. She had relied on the love of the father and mother for their son, and she felt sure that when once the thing was done they would take him back, and take her with him. They did nothing of the kind; they could not be induced to take him back. They forgave him, they said; but that was all, and one cannot live on forgiveness. They did not withdraw the little allowance they used to make him, but it was only a very little allowance. It would have kept a young bachelor well enough in London while he was making a career for himself; but it was nothing for a man with a wife who, in the very cigar shop itself, had acquired expensive tastes, and could understand no affection which did not frequently express itself in champagne. So they dragged on together, he still loving her in a sickly maniacal sort of way. She got champagne—sometimes from him when he had the money, sometimes from others. But she got the champagne, and she began to wear costly ornaments. Then he grew jealous, and she told him that she didn't care. A man had no right to marry, she told him bluntly, unless he had the means of keeping a wife according to her tastes. His people had deceived her, she said—they had taken her in; she never would have married him if she had known what horrid and hard-hearted people they were. But she meant to amuse herself in life, she declared; she had had enough of sentimentality.

"Did you never love me?" he asked, piteously. "Oh, love!—botheration!" was her encouraging reply, and then, further to relieve her feelings, she mentioned that she thought she was marrying a gentleman, and found she had married only a consumptive pauper. Even then he had not the courage to do anything; he told himself that he could not live without her. Very likely he could not. But he soon found that he certainly could not live with her. She deceived him for a time, then frankly ceased to deceive him, for she took no trouble to conceal anything from him. He died of consumption not long after, poor fellow! and his true friends were all glad that he had been set free. I had written a strong appeal to his father and mother, and with the dread of his death their anger melted away, and the mother wrote to say that they were both coming up to town to be near him. The letter came when I was standing beside his dead body in the presence of his wife. She took the letter and opened it. Her words summed up the situation. "Oh, bother!" she exclaimed; "what's the good of that now?"

Here was a little Marble Heart tragedy in Pickett's Place, off the Strand. I do not know what became of the Marble Heart. I never heard anything of the woman since. I never knew, in all my acquaintanceships, any instance of a promising, manly, generous life being so utterly and completely spoiled by an ignorant, selfish, and stupid little woman. Apart from all considerations of public improvement, I am glad that Pickett's

Place has gone. I am glad that it has gone, merely because I associated it always with her and with my unhappy friend. I am glad that it is gone, and the traffic of the Law Courts tramps every day over its all-but-forgotten grave.

V

THE LAW COURTS

WE are in the region of the Law Courts. The Law Courts have created here a region of their own—all their own. It is as when an army suddenly encamps in the close neighbourhood of some decaying old town— a new population, a new traffic, a new life quickly spring up about it like new vegetation. Mr. Pennell has made this very real for us in his sketches. He brings out with some vivid touches the character and colour of that new life which the Law Courts have created. We are standing in front of the entrances to the courts. Looking eastward we can see the matchless proportions of the mystical Griffin, and farther on the tower of St. Dunstan's. The tracery of the tower comes exquisitely out, and if one fixes his eyes on it and disdains for a moment the lower level of life, he might fancy himself back in some mediæval Nuremberg. People in general do not know how London can be glorified, etherealised, mysticised, utterly transfigured by looking from beneath up to its roofs and chimneys and gables. As we look at the tower of St. Dunstan's now we are easily lifted from the real into the ideal. St. Dunstan has long since lost his giants—so long since that many of the present generation of Londoners do not even know that St. Dunstan ever had giants to lose. "Before St. Mark still glow his steeds of brass," but before St. Dunstan no longer stand his Gog and Magog.

Come down, however, from St. Dunstan's and the clouds. Return to the Law Courts. "I mind the bigging o't," as poor Edie Ochiltree says in *The Antiquary*. I used to go to a newspaper office in the City a good deal about the time when the Courts were being built, and I took an interest in their progress, partly because of the long controversies in the House of Commons which had preluded the scheme for their erection — controversies as to site and structure and what not, which divided Parliament into hostile camps on the building question, as it had been divided years before on what I may perhaps call the constitution of South Kensington. The building of the Law Courts was destined to be the occasion of a different kind of controversy also, for there was a dispute with the workmen, and there was a strike, and there was the importation of foreign workmen to finish the buildings, and at one time the prophets of evil shook their heads and said the scheme had been unlucky from first to last, and the buildings would never be finished at all. The controversy, however, got settled somehow — that controversy; the Law Courts were built and opened. I remember the day well. The Queen in person presided over the ceremonial in the long narrow central hall.

It really was a magnificent pageant. I am not very fond of public ceremonials as a rule, but this was a noble sight. The order of the day was for men to wear either uniforms or Court dresses, except as regarded the Bar, of which the members wore the garb of their profession and its rank. No one was allowed to enter in ordinary morning dress—the few men who were not barristers and were not entitled to wear Court dress had to come in evening costume. Of course all the ladies were in full evening dress. I wonder if I may digress for a moment to mention a definition of the right to wear Court dress which was laid down for me once by lips that seemed to breathe forth authority? It was at a great dinner in the City—a feast given in honour of an eminent statesman and diplomatist. The cards of invitation prescribed that the guests were to come in uniform or Court dress. Nevertheless, there were several at the tables in ordinary evening garb. I got into talk with my next neighbour, who was evidently a civic dignitary

THE CORNER OF ESSEX STREET

of high rank, and we spoke on the subject of Court costume. I asked him how it happened that some gentlemen were allowed to come in ordinary evening dress. The truth is, I was smarting under a sense of wrong, for I had put myself into an antiquated Court suit which I had worn at a Speaker's dinner more than ten years before, and I had thus clad myself because I was under the impression that I should not be allowed in if I came in ordinary evening wear. My instructor said there had to be allowance made for gentlemen who, whatever their personal merits, were not entitled to put on Court dress. This opened a new field of inquiry to me, on which my friend was very willing to give me information. He explained to me all the various positions, dignities, offices, functions, acts and deeds, and so on, which entitled a man to put on Court costume. But I urged that surely a man who had not held any of these offices, or done any of these things, or gone through any of these presentation ceremonials, might nevertheless put on Court dress if he liked. My instructor settled the question at once, with dignity and even severity. "He might, sir," he said, "but it would be for him only fancy dress!" I questioned no more that day.

It was really a great ceremonial. One odd little incident of it made a fantastic impression on me. It was in the earliest days of December 1882. The late Archbishop of Canterbury had just died—was not yet buried. The ordinary spectators were arrayed along either side of the great hall, and there was kept open a wide space in the middle—a path by which the Queen and the Royal princes and princesses, and the great dignitaries of Church and State, were to pass to the places reserved for them. Suddenly there was borne along what seemed to be a sort of bier with a recumbent and deathlike figure in it. A shudder passed through some of those who stood near me, and some one in a loud whisper hazarded the explanation that, for some ancient reason or usage, it was held becoming that on such an occasion the last Archbishop of Canterbury, as well as his living successor, should be present. This, however, was not the true explanation. The true explanation was simple. One of the oldest of the judges was in such a condition of health that he could neither walk nor stand. He was unwilling, however, to remain away from the ceremonial, and he had himself thus borne into the hall. His pallid face and closed eyes, as he was carried past, gave some ground for the startling theory that we were looking on the bier of the dead Archbishop.

When the pageantry was over, and the Royal visitors had gone, the doors of the hall were thrown open for the general public, and the general public came in with a very ugly rush indeed. I have seen some crowding in my time, but I have seldom seen anything more formidable for the moment than that sudden meeting between the vast throng struggling to get in, and those who were still left in the hall struggling to get out. I was one of those who had remained in the hall, not knowing that the doors were to be thus suddenly thrown open; and I found myself, with my daughter, all at once in the thick of that terrible crowd. We were swept somehow out of the hall and on to the pavement. A few mounted police were striving to keep back some of the crowd, but the rush was too impetuous, and the force behind the nearest wave too great, to allow of any effectual restraint. I feared for a moment that the ill-luck of the Law Courts was about to be proved in a very ghastly way, and that lives would be lost in that terrible struggle. One poor girl—a nicely-dressed creature apparently of the sempstress class—fell down in a faint not far from where I was battling my way, and some men and women tumbled right over her; but they were up again in a moment, and they were trying to lift her— the very worst thing they could have done for her—when some police forced their way in and cleared a little space round the girl, and a kindly woman composed her arms and legs, and after a little she sighed and shivered and cried, and then came to all right again. Poor girl! the woman who attended her opened her firmly-clasped hand and found in it two sixpences—her little stock of funds, no doubt, for the day's holiday, and which even in her swoon she clutched firmly. After all there was no particular harm done to anybody so far as I could make out, but the danger for the moment was very genuine, and the horror of the situation remains clear in my memory. Nothing seems to me more pathetic and pitiful in its way than the half-crazy eagerness of the poorer class of Londoners to see any manner of sight. They will fight, struggle, rush, risk their lives, to see anything. Mothers will carry their little babies into the thick of the roughest crowd on the chance of having a glimpse at anything out of the common. Men and women will wait for hours in cold and rain to see a carriage drive by with some Royal personage in it. They will tramp for miles beside a handful of soldiers marching. The utter bareness and barrenness of their ordinary lives makes any novelty welcome to them. What did these men and women expect to see in the Law Courts that day? All the Royal visitors had been carefully got out of the way before the doors were thrown open. Nothing was to be seen but a long, narrow hall. Such a crowd would not care much about the hall's architectural merits. The hall could be seen the very next day by anybody. But there was the temptation—something, anything, to be seen at once—at once; and so they risked their limbs and their lives in the one mad overpowering desire to have a sight of it.

Two of the bravest and the coolest men I know or have ever known have alike told me that the one thing they most dread is the rush of a great crowd. Even a friendly crowd, I was told by each man, had a terror for him. I know a very plucky girl—and there are many girls a great deal pluckier than most men—who told me she never knew what fear was until she got involved in a great crowd at an election. It was a friendly crowd and a good-humoured crowd —would not willingly have hurt a hair of her head—but it was a crowd, and she was helpless to get out of it, and it was helpless to let her out, and she was painfully squeezed, and she saw nothing but the dense mass of coats and shawls and faces, and she felt as if she must faint, and asked herself what would happen to her if she fainted, and the crowd was eagerly rushing on and she was swept along with it; "and if I faint and fall," she thought, "they must rush over me and must trample me to death." I have seen her on the deck of a Levantine steamer in a white squall off Cape Matapan, and she showed no more fear than if she were at home in her drawing-room; but the election crowd was too much for her nerves, and she gave way to an utter terror.

I must say that I think a London crowd is almost always a good-natured crowd. Lately I passed through a London crowd which all the time I saw it was on a broad grin. There was a great function going on in the City, and a procession of carriages was driving along the Strand and Fleet Street. At either side and all along the route a dense wall of men and women, girls and boys, was set up. Every face was enlivened by the same broad grin. What was the source of the mirth? I could not guess—I have not the least idea. What did they see? Merely a string of carriages, with men and women in evening dress seated therein. No doubt some of us were ridiculous objects enough—that I readily admit. But we cannot all have been ridiculous. That pretty girl, now, so becomingly dressed, with the tall, handsome, soldierly-looking man, her father doubtless—what is there to laugh at in her, or in him, or in both together? Yet the grin was as broad while they were passing by as if they had been a pair of figures out of a Punch and Judy show. The mirth was not that of derision; it had nothing savage, nothing bitterly scornful about it. It was simply the expression of honest,

THE LAW COURTS

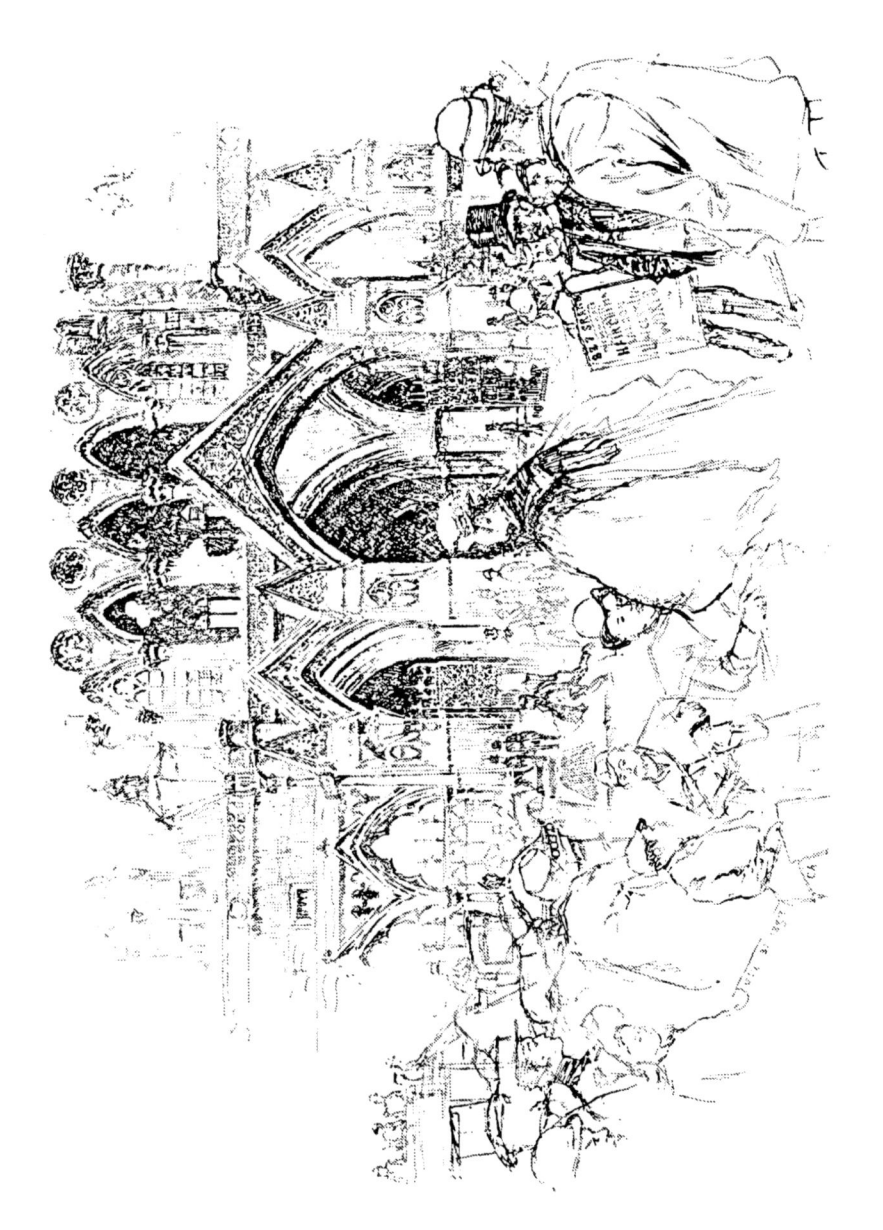

irrepressible amusement. For some reason or other we were all of us too much for that crowd—we were simply too ridiculous, and the crowd could not help itself—it must needs grin. It was trying, I confess, to be thus regarded as the laughing-stock of a good-natured crowd, which evidently did not want to offend or annoy us, but could not possibly keep from laughing at us. It was trying to have to pass slowly along through a mile or so of a throng every face in which was distended by this one unceasing and unchanging smile at us. Let us hope the ordeal may have done some of us good— may have helped to take the conceit out of us. It is not thus we are usually fond enough to regard ourselves—not as mere objects of the laughter of a crowd of our fellow-mortals. There can hardly be the self-conceit in man or woman which would not have some of the starch taken out of it by that promenade between those two lines of grinning faces. Mr. Pennell has drawn a flower-girl in one of these sketches. She is to be seen near the entrance to the Law Courts. She is a sonsie girl, with a broad mouth and a great smile: " Does she call all that a smile?"—I think I am quoting the words of some popular burlesque. It is a big smile, certainly, and I am sure that smile must have smiled *at* me, not *on* me, the day I had to face that singular ordeal. Well, she is a pleasant-looking girl, and I owe her no ill-will, even though she did honestly think me and my companions ridiculous creatures, and did frankly acknowledge the conviction by the distortion of her expressive countenance.

Observe the different types of lawyer which Mr. Pennell is able to show us. See that lawyer with the clean-shaven face; see that other with the moustache and beard and eye-glass. These are two contrasting types. The clean-shaven lawyer has his very soul in his profession. He has not a thought beyond it—he would not allow himself to have a thought beyond it, even if he could. He never reads anything but briefs and law reports. He never talks of anything but cases and verdicts and judgments. He has never been known to laugh at anything but one of his own jokes—of course in court—or any joke delivered by a judge. Elia says of himself that if the sun were some day to take to rising in the west and pursuing a steady course eastward, he, Elia, would never notice anything unusual in the reversed progress. Neither would our close-shaven lawyer, unless some one were to invite his attention to the phenomenon, and even then he would not trouble his mind long about it. Why should he? It would have no particular bearing on the case of Box *versus* Cox or Patter *versus* Clatter. How hard he works, our clean-shaven lawyer! He has a pull at his briefs late at night—last thing at night—and he is up early in the morning, and the moment he is cleanly shaven he goes at them again. I have seen him in a drawing-room after a dinner-party creep to a sofa and settle down there, and rest his head on the arm of the sofa and have a quiet little sleep—all from sheer physical exhaustion. Then in a few minutes he is awake and alert again. Now look at our other friend, the lawyer with the moustache and the beard and the eye-glass. He is an able man in his professional way too, but he does not surrender life absolutely to law and the Law Courts. Not he, indeed. Why, you can see by the first glance at him that he is a leading man in his Volunteer corps, that he is fond of rifle-shooting, that he likes to knock about the billiard-balls. You can see him on his horse in the Row every morning, and you may come upon him on a Sunday evening at Hurlingham, and there is seldom a first night of any importance in a London West-End theatre when he is not to be seen in one of the stalls. He enjoys life—he enjoys even his law cases; he is in good spirits about them; he takes them as a game, as an amusement, rather than as a duty and a business. But he never talks about them at a dinner-party —he will talk of anything else rather. Will he get on in his profession? Oh yes, he is getting on in his profession. There is no reason why he should not run his clean-shaven rival hard in the race. There are different ways of doing the same sort of work—of reaching the same end, that is all. Prince Hal takes to the battle in one spirit, Harry Hotspur in another. By the way, in Shakespeare's rendering it is Prince Hal who carries the day.

I admire the exterior of the Law Courts. I am told I ought not to do so, and that it is not the right thing to admire any part of the structure, outside or inside. But I cannot help myself—I cannot get over my invincible ignorance, and I stop every now and then in front of the Courts and look on them with admiration. I also admire the long, narrow hall. But my admiration comes to a stop there. Anything meaner, more uncomfortable, more ugly than the various little courts themselves, was never put together by the perverted ingenuity of man. It would be hard to exaggerate the utterly paradoxical character of these remarkable courts. They are too small; they are too large; they are too dark; they are too glaring; they are too hot; they are too cold; it is impossible to hear what a witness is saying, and yet each court is like a whispering gallery to send along the muttered gossip of some idle spectator. The draughts that howl through these rooms make one fancy he is in the Cave of Æolus. The great curtains which are hung at the doors are so arranged that they involve the hapless stranger trying to enter as if he were being rolled in a huge blanket. If you are seated securely in the court it is interesting to watch the struggles of this hapless stranger. You see his form bulging here and there through the thick drapery in which he has ignorantly invested himself. He thought he had nothing to do but to draw the curtain aside and go in: he did draw the curtain aside, but it took him into its folds and rolled itself round and round him, and look how he is struggling rightfully to be free! He plunges this way, and the curtain plunges with him; that way, and the curtain takes a new twist about him. At last he emerges, wrathful, shameful, his face red and glowing, and his hat—his poor hat, which he has had to carry in his hand through the thick of the fight! He knows that his face is dirty as well as red, for the curtain has clung to his bewildered countenance, and he is not without a fear that my Lord on the bench may have seen him, and may have thought he was doing it all for the fun of the thing, and perhaps may commit him for contempt of court. Contempt of court indeed! Who is there that could avoid feeling a contempt for that court? I speak, needless to say, of the chamber, not of the judges who are compelled to sit in it or the majesty of the law which they represent. I have heard judges themselves express over and over again their utter contempt for that court, even while they were sitting in it and administering justice. Indeed, the expression of their contempt was in itself an administration of justice.

I made an interesting acquaintance once in the precincts of these Law Courts. I made the acquaintance of a young barmaid. "Ye smile; I see ye, ye profane ones," as Byron says. She was occupied at one of the refreshment stalls near to a court which I used to have to attend. She was once a little distressed at the attentions of two young men somewhat of the 'Arry class. There was no one else there except myself, and she gave a pleading side-glance at me which told me beyond mistake or doubt that she wished me, and my graver and elder presence, to remain there until the 'Arries had taken their drink and gone their way. They did not mean to be rude, and they were not really rude in any offensive way, but they were chaffing each other about sweethearts, and then they began to ask her about her sweethearts, and she did not like it. They went away soon, and then she talked to me in the

ENTRANCE TO THE COURTS

frankest and most pleasant way. She was well-mannered and modest, and her talk was interesting. She told me she hardly ever met with any rudeness of any kind, but that she did not like being chaffed, and she was a little afraid of the two 'Arries. She did not know much about the business of the courts. She asked me if I was concerned in a case, and I said I was; and she asked me if it was something about property, and I said no—that it was not a civil matter at all—that it was a trial in a criminal court. She asked me if I was prosecuting some one, and I said no—some one was prosecuting me, which was perfectly true, for I was "had up" as a criminal conspirator. She was greatly puzzled, and evidently did not know how to reconcile my position with the favourable opinion she had allowed herself to form of me. I could see, however, that she was too good-hearted to permit any serious suspicion to invade her, and that she took it for granted there must be some reputable explanation. I did not see her again for months. My next appearance in court was, as Mr. Micawber puts it, "in the capacity of defendant in Civil process." I went to the refreshment stall again and saw my friend. She was pleased to see me, and asked how I had got on in my former case, and I told her I had got off, which again a little puzzled her, and that this time I was only mixed up in a civil case. She wished me luck in that too, and I thanked her and felt thankful. She asked me if I had just come to town, and whether the weather was fine in my part of the country. She was naturally under the impression that I only came up to town every now and then to bear a part in some law case. We had some pleasant talk together, and I left her with a kindly feeling, regarding her as a friendly, fresh, intelligent, and lady-like girl. She has for me another interest, too, in the fact that she is the only barmaid with whom, so far as I can remember, I ever exchanged a single word that did not belong strictly to the business of my demand and her supply. I do not believe that I ever before got even so far into conversation with a young lady at a refreshment counter as to hazard a remark on the fairness or the foulness of the weather.

In front of the Griffin the traffic gets all crowded together. A policeman stands dignified and motionless in the midst of it—a grand sight. Nothing disturbs him. The waves seem to beat on him in vain. He stands like the Eddystone Lighthouse in a storm. He seems, however, to be, unlike the Eddystone, somewhat conscious of the dignity of his position and his demeanour. How, indeed, could he possibly be unconscious of the one and the other? He can stop all that movement of traffic with a wave of his majestic hand. He could say to that stream of omnibuses, "Thus far, and no farther—for the moment—until I bid you go forward again." He can give pause to that swift-darting hansom, whose occupant, craning over the doors with eager, impatient gaze, is evidently bent on trying to catch some train. But, no—whether he catch the train or miss it, there must his cab stand motionless until the steadfast policeman sets it free to go its way. Even that stately carriage, with the splendid footmen and the two elegantly-dressed ladies who recline on its cushions—even that must stand when he commands. He is not without respect and even reverence, in a way, for carriages and their owners, but when duty has to be done he can be as severe with a coroneted barouche as with a donkey-cart. I always think that the traffic-directing policeman in the middle of the roadway has one distinct advantage over the policeman promenading along the footpath in the fact that he is not asked many questions. One could not stop in the midway of that torrent of traffic to ask the policeman anything. But the officer on the sidewalk, how he is beset with questions! You see him in Mr. Pennell's sketches just as you may see him every day in real life,

THE CLOCK TOWER OF THE LAW COURTS

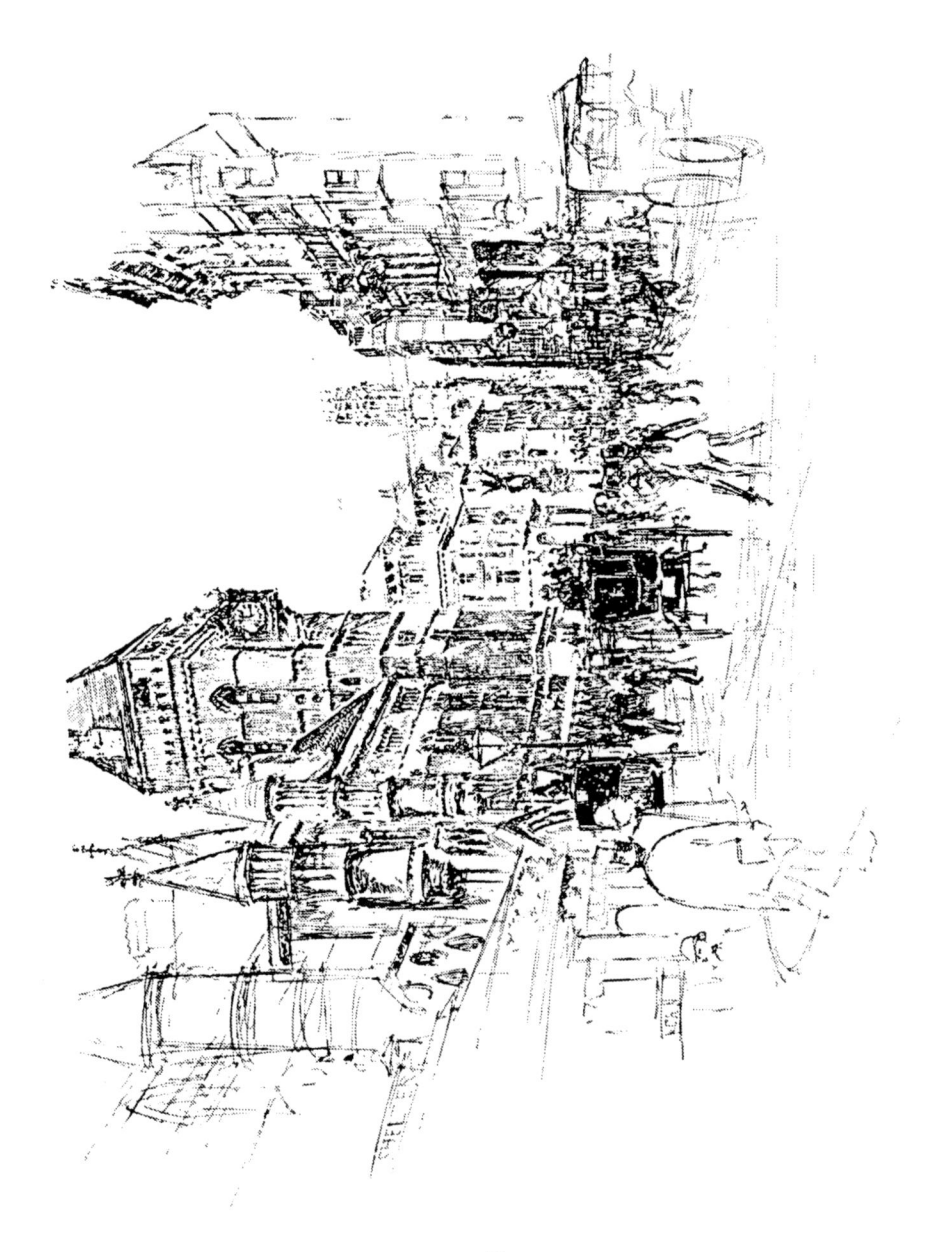

with his head bent down to catch the purport of some little woman's interrogatory. It must be trying to be stopped in the middle of Fleet Street and invited to point out the shortest way to Shepherd's Bush, or Longridge Road, South Kensington, or how to get to the School of Cookery. But I never saw a policeman look impatient or heard of his giving other than a civil answer. His resources of memory and self-possession never fail him. When anybody stops me in the street and suddenly asks me the way to any place, I instantly lose my head and forget where the place is, or how to get to it, even though it should happen to be in some spot quite close to my own abode.

Let us go back into the Law Courts and enter any one of them. It is marvellous the manner in which, by mere listening, one can bring himself to take an interest in anything. Here is a claim for damages being heard. A man has been knocked down by an omnibus—he was not very severely hurt, and there is nothing at all of the tragical about his story. But he was put out of work for a time and had to pay a doctor, and so he makes his claim; and the omnibus company dispute it, and insist that it was all his own fault and his own carelessness, and the learned counsel on both sides fight the quarrel out. You listen and you become strangely interested. Gradually you grow to be quite a partisan—of the omnibus, or the man, as the case may be. You think the little jokes of the counsel are quite refreshing, and as for the judge, when he condescends to be merry with one of the witnesses, you find yourself breaking into a peal of laughter. Next day you look out in the papers for a report of the case, and are very much disappointed when you find it compressed into about six lines, which six lines are published, it would seem, mainly for the purpose of giving the names of the learned counsel. Then one begins to understand why it is that courts of law have their regular attendants, who resort there not because of some particular case in which they feel an interest, but simply because the courts are open and something is going on. I have noticed that some people come regularly to the same court day after day, bringing a packet of sandwiches with them, which they consume at the regular luncheon-time, remaining in the court while all others have gone out, and while I am eating something at the refreshment-bar and talking to my one and only friend there. How do they live, these people who come day after day to the courts? They cannot all be persons of property—none of them look quite like that—and how and when do they work for their living? What can the occupations be which allow men to devote the greater part of the day to the unprofitable pastime of attending the sittings of a law court? They cannot all be printers on the staff of a morning paper; they do not look like actors; they cannot all belong to my line of life and do literary work at night; and there they are day after day, day after day! They are of kin, apparently, with the poorly-dressed men who sit in St. James's Park for hours daily. I suppose the men and women who attend the courts get to feel as if they were acquaintances of the officials, and of the counsel, and even of the judges. They do, I know, sometimes pick up an acquaintance which may ripen into something like friendship with certain of the policemen and the ushers. One can fancy some such regular visitor at the courts sitting in St. James's Park one day during the long vacation with his little boy or girl, and seeing a dignified-looking person pass by who graciously salutes him with a nod of the head. "Who is that gentleman, papa?" "That gentleman, my dear, is Mr. Wafer, usher in the Lord Chief Justice's court; he is a very particular friend of mine." How proud that child feels of that parent! How proud that parent feels of himself! It would be worth sitting in court for months of the dullest cases to win at the end the triumph of such a moment! We can all bring it home to ourselves easily enough. You are walking in Hyde Park on a Sunday with your admiring niece from the country. Some one salutes you graciously. "Uncle, who is that gentleman?" "That, my dear, is the Lord Chief Justice"—or Lord Wolseley, as the case may be. Then we do, indeed, feel that life is worth living, and that we in particular have not lived in vain. The one touch of nature makes the whole world kin.

VI

FLEET STREET

FROM the new realms of the Law Courts we get into the ancient region of the newspapers. It is ancient, of course, only in a sense. It was not particularly noted as a newspaper region about the time when Dr. Johnson invited Boswell to take that famous walk down Fleet Street. But it seems ancient to us now, and Fleet Street is as much the accepted and typical region of the newspaper and the newspaper man as the Latin Quarter was once, and even to some extent still is, the recognised home of the Bohemian student. Mr. Pennell gives us some well-chosen glimpses of this region. Look at the two opposite corners of that little lane

BANK

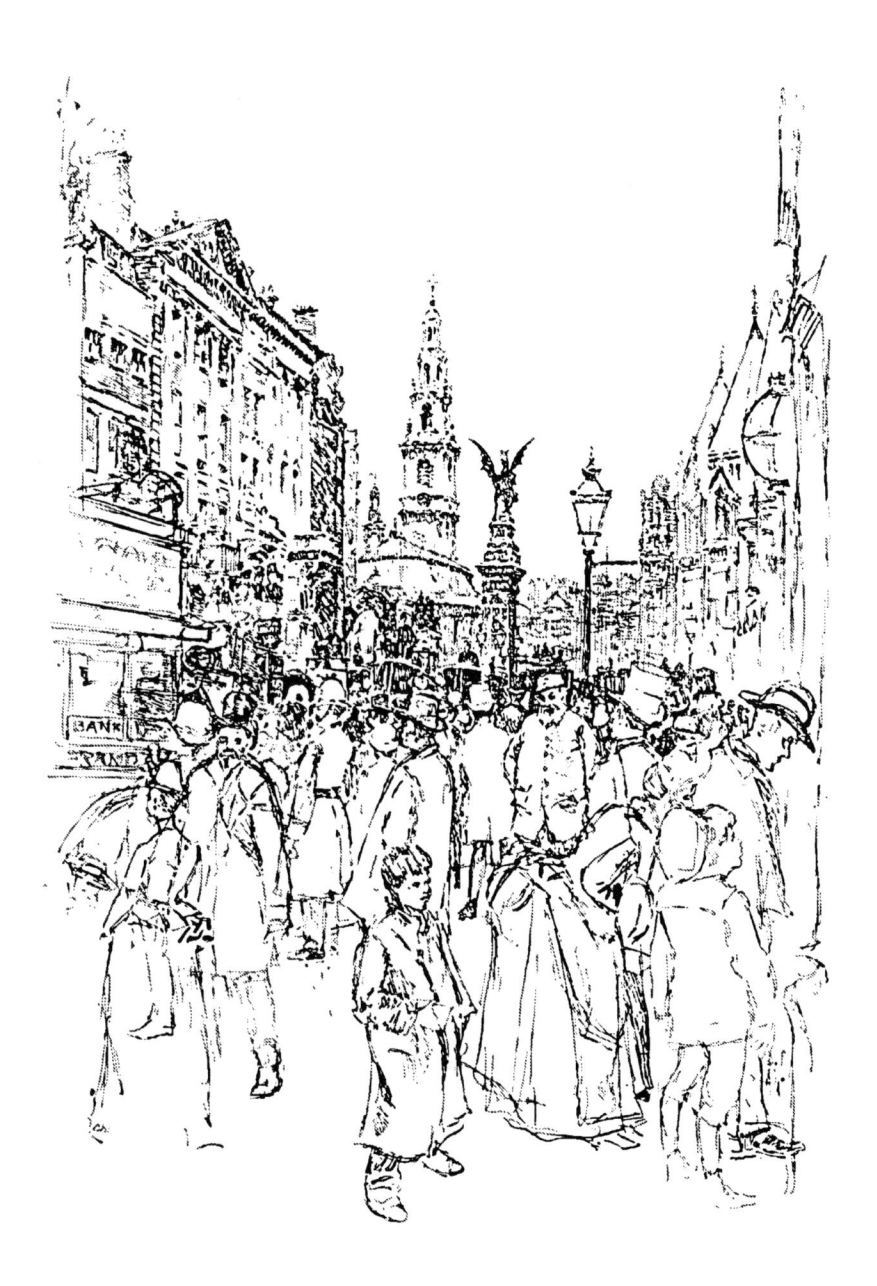

FLEET STREET

which opens out from Fleet Street: one corner occupied by the *Punch* office, the other by the office of the *World*. One cannot now imagine a London without *Punch*. It seems curious to think that such a publication should ever have been called the London *Charivari*; so little of the *Charivari* is, or ever was, about thoroughly English Mr. Punch. Never from first to last was there a flavour of anything that was not thoroughly British about Mr. Punch: his prejudices—and what prejudices he did show now and again!—were thoroughly English. But how healthy, pure, and manly his humour always! A Paris comic paper makes its stock-in-trade of one subject only—illicit love. Mr. Punch never saw any fun in the fact that a husband was deceiving his fond wife, or that a wife was carrying on an intrigue with her credulous husband's closest friend. Mr. Punch could have been as droll about this as any Frenchman of them all if he saw any fun or drollery in it; but, bless his honest, manly heart! he did not, and we are all greatly obliged to him for it. Mr. Punch started as a rather extreme Radical in the days of Douglas Jerrold and Tom Hood and Thackeray. He went in a good deal for the "man-and-a-brother" principle; he was much in sympathy with the *prolétaire*. One of his many ephemeral rivals satirised him, I remember, by publishing the titles of various poems humorously alleged to have appeared in the pages of *Punch*— "Sit down by me, my shoeless brother"; "Come, share my lodging, honest tramp," and such like; but Mr. Punch soon got out of that humour, and no one could think of satirising him after that fashion now. But the praise that I have given *Punch* no enemy could deny him. During all his long reign he has had genius and art to help him, and he has had purity too. See what a crowd is peering into his windows, where you behold the pages of far-back numbers displayed, and may study a caricature of "Pam," or of "Dizzy," or even of Brougham and O'Connell. Some of the cartoons must surely be a rare

ST. DUNSTAN'S IN THE WEST

puzzle to the schoolboys who stare at them through the windows; there are members of Parliament, doubtless, who would at this hour be unable to explain the meaning of this or that humorous grouping; but the drawing is always so admirable and so full of life and movement that people look at it and stick to it for its own sake. I always stop at that *Punch* corner, and try to get close up to the window-pane and stare delighted.

At the other side of the little court stands the *World* office. The glimpse of that little court is a pretty picture. One gets a sudden, unexpected impression of trees and old houses, and the stone tower of a church. The church tower looks ancient and time-honoured—a little out of keeping, seemingly, with the modern humours of Mr. Punch and the Society gossip of *Atlas*. But there is really no incongruity; life is all like that, and would be much less interesting if it were not so. Take the oldest and most venerable church in England; when it was in its youth there was satirical talk and Society gossip going on under the shadow of its spires and towers. That which it was familiar with in its youth it need not be ashamed at in its old age. The *World*, too, was like *Punch* an

THE WINDOWS OF "PUNCH"

innovation. Like *Punch*, it had numerous imitators and rivals who soon dropped out of rivalry, and some who still hold on in the competition. The *World* started, for England, the popular and personal Society

WORLD

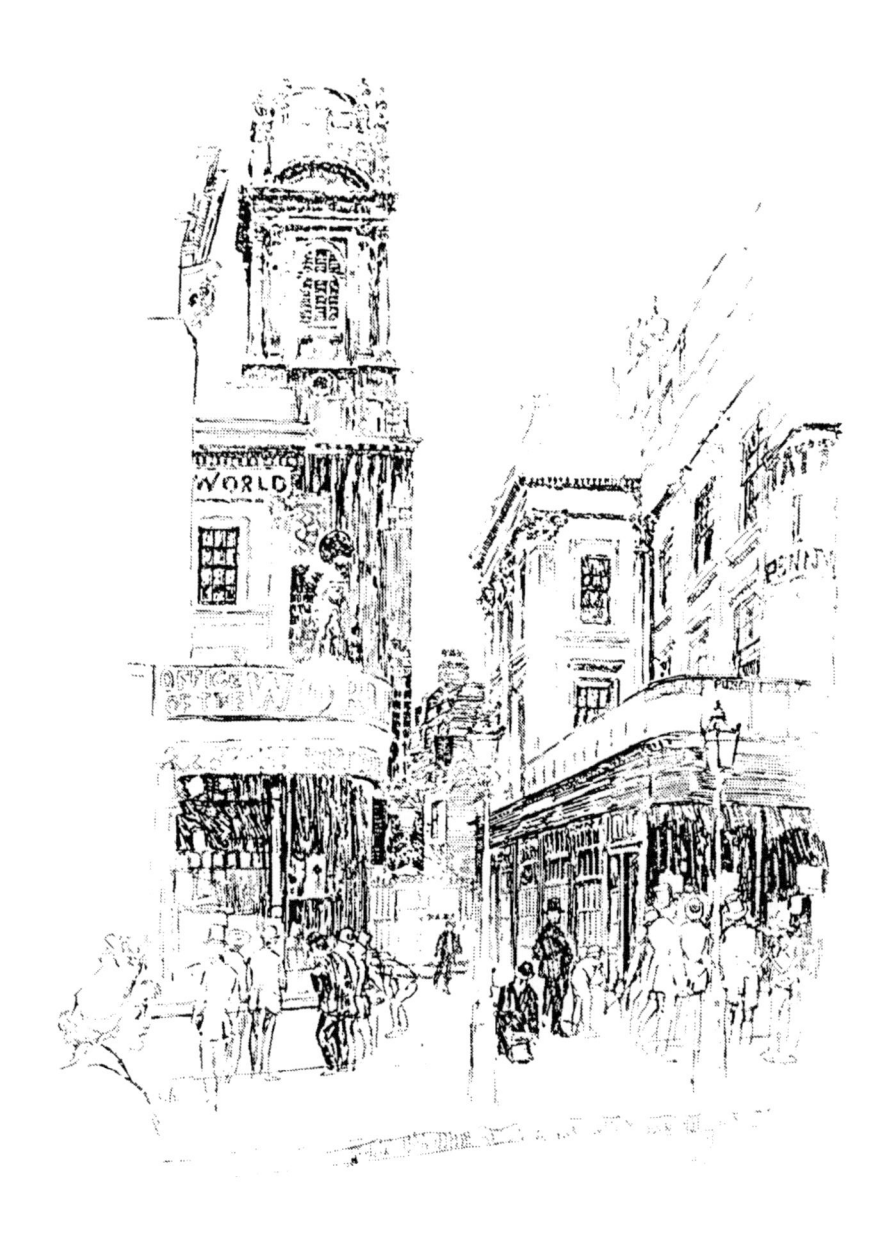

ST. BRIDE'S PASSAGE

O

journal. The *Owl* was altogether a different sort of thing; it was very clever and very brilliant, no doubt, but its cleverness and brilliancy were meant for the circles which have the Foreign Office as their centre, while *Atlas* naturally appeals *urbi et orbi*, to all. I do not often agree with the political opinions of the *World*, but one must recognise the fact that here is a clever Society paper which a young woman may read. Gossip—personal gossip? No doubt personal gossip is an objectionable thing from the point of view of the higher morality; and of course the point of view of the higher morality ought to be the point of view of every one of us. Only it is not. And we do nearly all of us indulge, and even delight, in personal gossip, even when it is spiced with a little scandal. Is it not something, then, to have our personal gossip served up to us by clever men—and I suppose I may say by clever women—by men and women of education, who understand and instinctively feel where the line ought to be drawn, and to whom it comes natural to distinguish between the gossip which causes a smile and the gossip which compels a blush? I daresay I should feel loftily proud of my austere virtue if I could declare with truth (or concerning "Truth,") that I never read these Society papers. But I do read them, and shall continue doing so—and go to, then!

More of the boyish population crowd around the windows of *Punch* than around the panes of the *World*. *Punch* has cartoons, the *World* has none; and the boy, as a rule, takes but slight interest in the doings of Belgravia, and the Court drawing-rooms, and the interchange of friendly *badinage* between "Edmund" and "Henry." But observe the totally different sort of crowd around the windows of the *Sporting News*! What a number of billycock hats! and what an expressive article of headgear the billycock hat becomes on the head of a Londoner! Look at the open-mouthed hobbledehoy with his hands thrust loosely into his pockets! Every hat is expressive, but I think the

OAP
1471

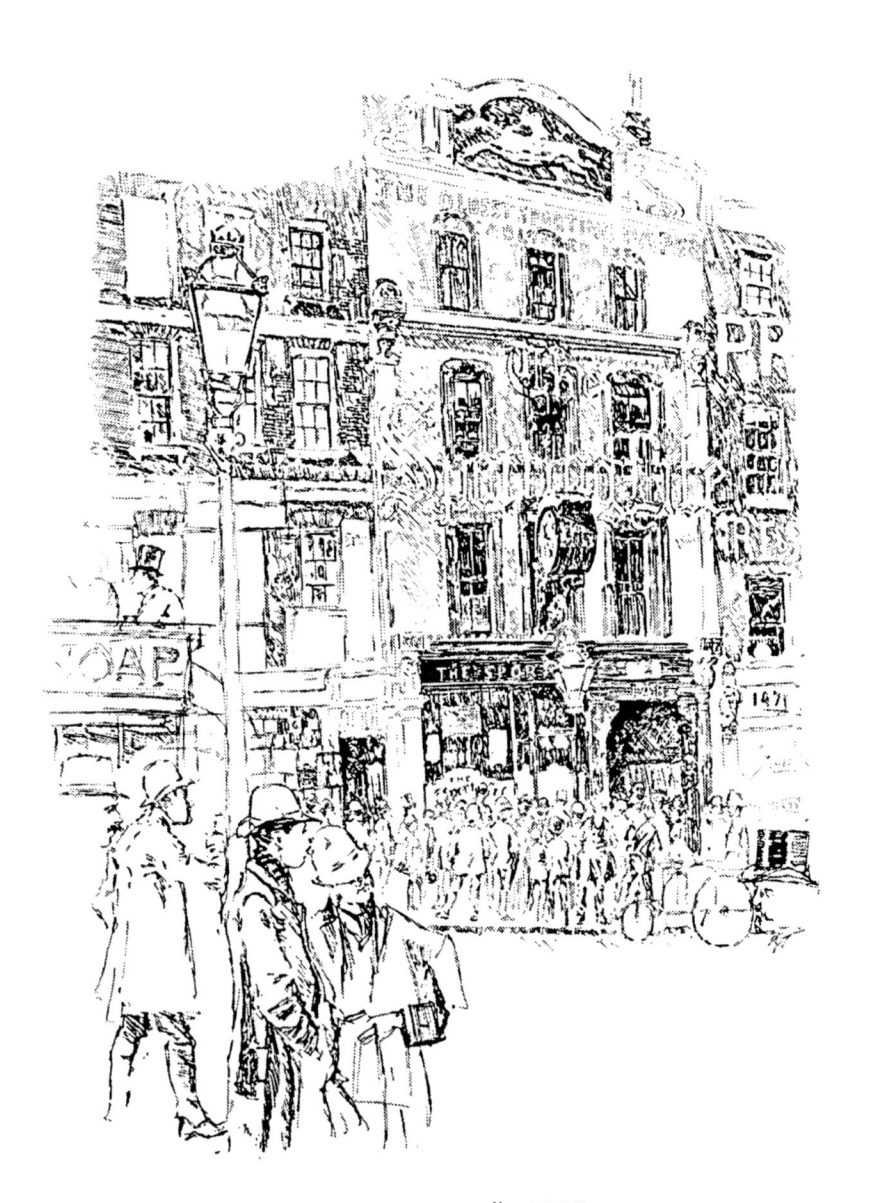

"SPORTING LIFE" OFFICE

billycock tells its story best of all. The
shovel hat may deceive; it may sometimes—
not to speak irreverently—cover the brows
that a billycock would have more appropri-
ately adorned. Many of the curiously antiquated hats worn by ancient members of the
House of Peers may likewise lend themselves
to an imposition. There may now and then
be levity, frivolity, a very passion for idle
amusement, concealed beneath these relics of
the past. I have often wondered, by the way,
where these aged peers get these "quaint
and olden" hats! No man now sees such a
headpiece in a hatter's shop. Do the aged
peers insist on having the hats specially built
for them after some venerable fantasy of their
own? Or did it happen that in various cases a
young nobleman of the time of D'Orsay or
Tom Duncombe's brightest years, or Lynd-
hurst's dressy days, was smitten with a passion
for some particular beaver, and vowed that he
would wear that pattern, and that pattern
only, till death did him and it part? Then did
each man go to his hatter and leave with him

a pattern, and insist that that, and that alone, must be supplied to him during the rest of his existence? It may be so; we all know about the shepherd's-plaid trousers which were repeated and reproduced for Brougham while generations of perpetual change rolled on. Count Cavour was intensely fond of one costume—a snuff-coloured swallowtail, with trousers and waistcoat to correspond: his tailor had instructions to supply him with that costume, and that costume only. Perhaps the hats of the ancient peers are furnished on the same principle. But I have wandered far from the *Sporting Life* and the billycock to the House of Lords and its old-world hats, and even to the arcades of Turin and the snuff-coloured coat of the great Cavour.

Then there is the office of the *Daily News*, the advertising and selling office—the office in Fleet Street. An eager crowd has gathered in front of its windows—some important news has been placarded; but it is an earnest crowd, with not many boys or billycocks in it. How these Fleet Street newspaper offices are making Fleet Street a palatial thoroughfare in our days! The *Telegraph*, the *Standard*, the *Chronicle*—they are like some of the great American newspaper offices in vastness, in arrangement, and in splendour. Admiring all these, however, yet let me be allowed to tell of the positive fascination wrought upon me by one collection of old houses a little more westward in Fleet Street, which appear to be a very rookery of newspaper offices and all manner of public institutions. These houses are very old. They are highly picturesque. No doubt they are as firm and staunch and strong as they are old; but that is not the impression given to the ignorant and superficial gazer— to me, for example. They seem marked out and "girdled" for speedy demolition. The odd thought comes into the mind that the various newspaper agents have simply taken possession of them as squatting families have settled down in ruined piles; or that the newspapers have swooped on them only for the purpose of hanging out each his banner on the outward walls for the business of advertisement. I read the names of famous provincial journals—of musical journals; I read, too, of various companies and institutions; and I read of somebody's oyster-rooms. The whole place looks oddly like a dilapidated hive. These houses will be pulled down probably some early day, and handsome structures will grow up in their stead. Then the great provincial newspaper offices, and the offices of the musical journals, and the companies and institutions, will look quite in their right place, and there will be no incongruous suggestion of progress and prosperity taking up their home among ruins. But will the sight be quite so picturesque then for the searching Doctor Syntax of the London streets? Perhaps not. The incongruous is surely very often an important element in the creation of the picturesque.

An elderly man, in a deer-stalker hat, is seen about this part of the street. I mean he is seen in Mr. Pennell's sketch, and Mr. Pennell's sketch is just as good as the street

The
DAILY
NEWS
OFFICE
FOR
67 The DAILY NEWS
67
Daily News
DAILY NEWS
67

"DAILY NEWS" OFFICE

—just as real as the street. I know that elderly man, but he does not come from Sheffield, in the sense of the phrase which belongs to that popular piece, "A Pair of Spectacles." I know the man—at least, I know the kind of man. His face was handsome, it is still delicate and refined; a little wasted, a little pinched even, but "cheery still," like Abou-ben-Adhem, may whose tribe increase! Our friend in the deerstalker has had some trouble in his time. Henry of Navarre said of himself that the wind of adversity blowing early and long in his face turned his hair prematurely white. So it has evidently been with our friend. His has a gentle, subdued expression about his eyes and lips. He has not got on well in life. He has a wife and a large family—all daughters. His is exactly the appearance of a man who has only daughters. He is intensely fond of his wife and the girls, and his wife and the girls are intensely fond of him. But the girls still believe in him, and the wife has long since, gently and considerately, ceased to do so. When I say she has ceased to believe in him, I mean that she has ceased to believe in his projects and in his capacity for success. As to his personal integrity, his unselfishness, and his love, her faith in him has waxed rather than waned since the day they were married, at the time when every one said he was a rising young man certain to get on. But she no longer believes in his plans, his projects, his new ways of making money— she has outlived too many of them. She is resigned, however, and is happy, knowing his worth. The girls have still the fullest, and even the proudest, faith in everything he undertakes. They will probably all get married—they are just the girls whom sensible and honest young men would like to marry—and papa will always be a hero to them. Poor dear man! he is a failure in many ways—in most ways—but not in all. A man cannot be said to have wholly failed in life whose wife loves him to the last, and who is always a hero in the eyes of his daughters. There are many great worldly successes not quite so enviable as that.

The traffic becomes perplexed, seemingly inextricable, seemingly impossible, as we get on towards Ludgate Circus. I have already tried to do justice to the heroic figure of the policeman, standing in the midst of the rush and surge and swirl, upright and motionless, like the Eddystone amid the stormy waves. Let me try to describe another heroic figure of a different kind. Be pleased to look at that omnibus trying to thread its way through that moving mass of horses, wheels, and men. Where is that omnibus to get to? How can it edge itself in any farther? It must come into collision with something; it must upset something or be upset—perhaps upset *and* be upset. It is leaning over ominously to one side already, like a sailing yacht in a squall. Now look at the driver seated on his box. Does he seem dismayed? Does he seem even anxious? Not he! He is listening with an air of keen and wide-awake interest to something that a passenger on the box-seat is telling him. Perhaps it is a good story, and there is a whimsical expression on the driver's face which would seem to warrant such an assumption. Anyhow his attention appears to be all absorbed in the story, or whatever it is, as if the worst perils of the traffic had no concern for him; as if no one had ever heard of a collision in the streets of the City. But do you suppose that he has not his eyes and enough of his mind on the traffic, and on his own task? Of course he has. He knows what he is about. Half an eye is enough for him. He is master of his subject. He can spare ear and interest enough for the talk of his companion; he misses not a point of it: but he can mind his own business all the time. No collision for him; he will upset nothing, and be upset by nothing. Now, this is a different kind of heroic figure from the other. There are heroes who are silent, stern, unmoved on the battlefield, wholly wrapped up in the business of battle. There are heroes who must take battle itself easily and lightly, and who can make or enjoy a joke at the moment when preparing to charge. Let us recognise the heroism of both orders of hero, and just feel a preference according to our own personal inclination. I invite no decision between my grave and statuesque policeman and my easy, happy-go-lucky omnibus-driver. Each is a characteristic figure of the London streets, and each has been given to us by Mr. Pennell with a fidelity and sympathy which is in itself an inspiration. Each is given to us in his habit as he lives, just as you may see him in the City every day.

Fleet Street is all contrasts, for any one who will only allow a little ray of fancy to help him with its divining light. We have seen our heroic policeman and our heroic cabman. Now let us cast a glance at that trim little milliner with her two bundles. She trips along bravely through all "the thunderous smother"—the phrase, I think, is from a poem of Leigh Hunt's—and it does not disturb her nerves in the least. But the contrast I was going to draw is not between her and anybody else—I was only going to say that the office of Messrs. Cook has just come into sight. You don't see the contrast. You ask, "What contrast?" There is the most home-keeping creature in London perhaps, and yonder is Cook's Tourist's Office, where you can take a ticket to go anywhere over the world or round the world. For any one with an inborn love of travel to go into such an office is as tantalising as to ramble among the Liverpool docks or along the quays of Marseilles, and see the vessels that are coming from and going to the far-off ports to which one's yearning heart and fancy strain. That tourist office is tapestried with announcements of return tickets to and from all the famous places of the globe. The Rhine? Well, the name of the Rhine makes one melancholy, for the world of to-day has wellnigh forgotten the Rhine. Byron sang of it; Disraeli apostrophised it in passionate rhetoric, wherein he appealed to it as "River of my youth!"—and the Rhine is as lovely as ever—and who raves about it now? Alas! rivers come into fashion and go out of it, like other things. Switzerland, of course, Italy, the Danube, the Bosphorus, the Nile, the Holy Land, India, Japan, China. Ah! what delightful and yet torturing invitations to some who cannot accept them! But our little milliner now— she would not care. She does not want to see Karnak and the Tombs of the Kings: the name of the Taj-Mahal awakens in her mind no manner of interest. She would hate the idea of being packed off to China or Japan. The passion for travel, for wandering, for seeing new places, is in the breast of every boy; but girls do not, as a rule, take any interest in "Sinbad the Sailor." Some women of education do, indeed, get a passion for travel and even for exploring. Most of us know women who have made themselves famous as travellers and even as explorers. But to the ordinary girl, even to the ordinary educated girl, much travel is a mere bore. As for our little milliner, the idea of travelling abroad never entered into her head. What would be the good if it did? How could she travel? Yet the same would apply to her young man, her sweetheart—and we may be sure he never passes Cook's or Gaze's office without lingering long and longingly at the windows, and studying the announcements, and sighing with a desire to have a ticket for everywhere. He and the little milliner have been to Greenwich and to Epping, and that is travel enough for her. But he yearns for something farther off, and perhaps when they are married and doing pretty well he may take her for a little trip to Dieppe and to Paris. We may be sure that the impulse will be his and not hers—that he will delight in the trip and she will put up with it.

VII

LUDGATE HILL

THE railway bridge that crosses Ludgate Hill was once the occasion of a fierce controversy. It was a struggle between the artistic and the practical—between the æsthetic and the economic. It was the old controversy—not quite so old as the hills, but certainly as old as the very first time when industrial science of the rudest form began to turn the hills to account for the supposed benefit of man. Why, then, should not Ludgate Hill come on for her turn in the discussion? Ludgate Hill "waited for her time—which time came," as Carlyle says, discoursing on a quite different subject. The time came when it was proposed to span Ludgate Hill with this railway bridge. As may be seen by Mr. Pennell's sketch, the railway bridge itself is

THE RAILWAY BRIDGE, LUDGATE HILL

by no means an unlovely object. Regarded as a railway bridge merely, it is rather a fine work of art. Its iron tracery is delicate and picturesque. But then, as a bridge crossing

Ludgate Hill and cutting off from Fleet Street the view of St. Paul's—how about it when considered in that way? Thus the controversy arose. Mr. Ruskin struck in with characteristic gallantry, and condemned the practical principle which would spoil so fine a street view for the convenience of a railway and its passengers. I remember favouring the public with some opinions of my own on the same subject in a newspaper with which I was then connected, and which newspaper I have long outlived. My opinions merely said ditto to Mr. Ruskin. Yes, it was a fine street view—one of the finest street views in London—which met the eyes of those who looked up from Fleet Street to Ludgate Hill and St. Paul's. It was a grand historic sight. Many of the old houses were still standing, and the whole scene retained much of its mediæval aspect. Let it be frankly owned that the view is spoiled now—utterly spoiled. The railway bridge bounds the horizon of one walking from Fleet Street. He sees nothing but that; thinks of nothing but that. Perhaps I should rather put it this way—he hardly sees the bridge, for he does not think about it; but he sees nothing, also, and thinks of nothing. Now, in the old days, a goodly proportion of the wayfarers could hardly fail to be struck by the hill, and the Cathedral on its brow. But then the men of practical progress, even if they are willing to admit all this, will ask us what are the artistic or æsthetic glimpses of a few visionaries and dreamers when compared with the comfort and the convenience of the thousands and thousands who pass along in the railway, backwards and forwards, every day?

There it is, you see. If the controversy were to go on all over again, I should not take part in it. Not that I have changed my opinions in the least as to the general principle or as to this particular instance. But where is the good of arguing on such a subject? The artistic always goes down before what is called the practical in a matter like that. "Keep your breath to cool your

LUDGATE CIRCUS

porridge," was a good old Scottish proverb. Keep your controversial ardour for something in which it may possibly prevail. Against railway bridges, and telegraph wires, and other such works, it is of no account. Against the genius of street placard and advertisement it is of no account. The most beautiful and venerable parts of our most venerable and stately structures must be accounted as of nothing when the genius of Civilisation has need of a blow-hole on the road hard by. We are not worse than other civilised peoples. We are only doing as the Romans do—observe the recent improvements in what a Complete Letter-writer calls "the Imperial City of the Cæsars." There will be tramways in Jerusalem yet—perhaps there are such already; some years have passed since I was in Jerusalem. Does any one know a lovelier river than the Hudson, about West Point? I do not. But the rocks on the margin are utilised for the purpose of advertising in flaring characters the virtues of this man's bitters and that other man's pills. Therefore I, for one, give up the fight. Let Mr. Ruskin battle on; he is "possessed," in the demoniac sense, by a principle; he has a mission. I would encourage him and wish him success, if there were the slightest hope; but there is not. So why should London wait—for the effacing and reconstructing fingers of modern utility? Let them efface; let them reconstruct. Some of us can still see in memory the Ludgate Hill that was. Most of us do not care what it was, or what it is, or what it is to be. But I may be allowed to express a little regret that Mr. Pennell did not see it and sketch it before the beginning of the process which is to improve it "from the face of all creation— off the face of all creation." Some words which I read lately in a most touching story by M. Anatole France, come back to my memory poignantly: "I grow sad, sometimes," says the noble old scholar who is supposed to tell the story, "to think that the effort which we make—we cultured persons, so called—to retain and preserve dead things is a weary and a vain effort. All that has lived is the necessary aliment of new existences. The Arab who builds himself a hut with the marbles of the temples of Palmyra is more philosophic than all the conservators of the museums of London, of Paris, and of Munich." So says the venerable hero of "The crime of Silvestre Bonnard, Member of the Institute." Then what a philosopher was the Turk who, like a practical soldier, used the pillars and statues of the Parthenon as targets! But dear old M. Bonnard did not mean what he said. He was in a mood of despondency—a mood of despair. He was giving up the fight he had fought so long in vain. He had not Mr. Ruskin's mission. He threw down his broken sword, but could not resist the temptation to fling a few words of sarcasm and scorn in the face of the conquering Utility.

What a turmoil there is about Ludgate Circus! What roofs, what telegraph wires —what placards, ensigns, advertisements high in air—what omnibuses, carriages, carts, cabs, donkey-carts, the cart which the costermonger pushes before him, the mail-carts, the carts of the *Star* newspaper, equally red with those of Her Majesty's mail, the oblong carts of the Parcel Post—all these are on the earth, and make the firm ground look like a quaking bog. The great signs that are hung out across the fronts of houses, and on the tops of houses, make Ludgate Circus look like a part of New York. The Obelisk rises out of the throng in the street like a solitary camel's head out of the crowd of a pilgrimage. The spire rising out of the pell-mell has more significance. It invites us all to look up—up—above "the city's rout and noise and humming." I wonder how many wayfarers in each day are touched by the appeal of the spire and look upwards! I wonder how many who do look upwards are impelled thereto by the spire's silent admonition, and are the better for it! That man yonder now—he is looking up. He is gazing upwards

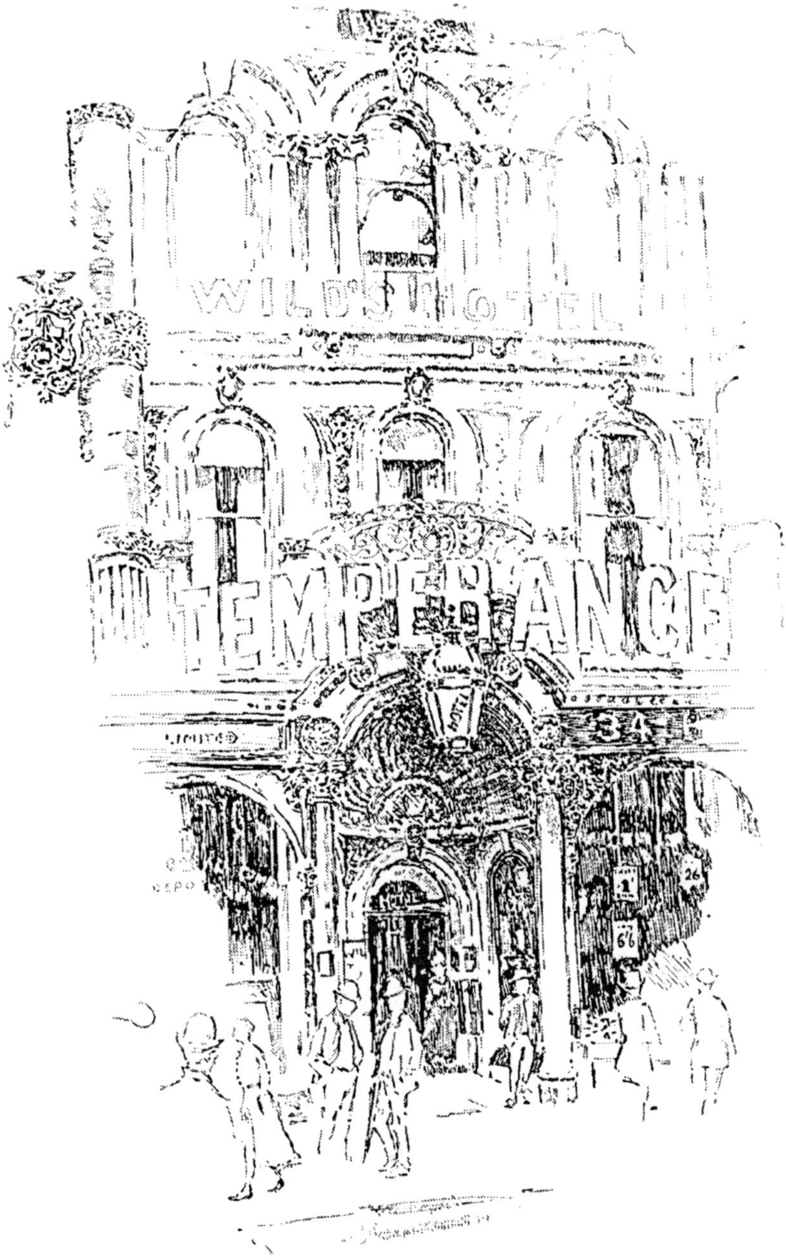
WILD'S HOTEL
TEMPERANCE
34
LIMITED

WILD'S HOTEL

very earnestly—so earnestly that he runs into the chest of a rough-looking person in a fur cap, who is walking westward and striving the while to keep his eyes on something eastward. The two collide, and our skygazer makes an apology which sounds like an imprecation. Was that all the lesson he learned from the teaching of the church spire? No; he would have learned something better if he had sought teaching there. But he was only looking up to the sky to see if it was going to rain. He was put into a bad humour by the ominous aspect of the closing and darkening clouds, and so when the chance collision took place he was in the mood for an imprecation. By the way, do not look for the men or the collision in Mr. Pennell's sketch; they are my own invention. Mr. Pennell's pencil is too good to be employed in working out such poor conceits.

The only thing worth noticing in this poor conceit is that it illustrates a peculiarity of the London streets, which I have long been observing with a certain interest.

Along London pavements—and I suppose the pavements of other cities as well—the men and women of what I may call, for want of any better term, the educated classes, walk straight on with their eyes to the front of them. If they want to look into a shop window they stop in their walk, go up to the shop window, and look into it. But while they are on the march they look before them. Now observe the men and women, the lads and lasses, of what we must call, for lack of a better word, the uneducated class. You will observe that five out of every six of them are walking one way and looking another way. Something a little distance behind him has caught a man's attention. It may be an organ and a monkey, it may be an Oriental foreigner, it may be an upset hansom or a fallen horse, it may be anything. He cannot take his eyes from it, and so he keeps on walking backwards. He is moving, indeed, towards his destination, but he still looks back to that he has left behind him. Observe Mary Jane—or shall we say Betsinda?—with her perambulator and her two young charges. She drives them on directly, recklessly, remorselessly; but all the time her eyes are with her heart, and that is in the shop windows, where all the beautiful, beautiful things are displayed for sale—the bonnets, the unmade-up silks, the mantles of stamped velvet, the gauzy dresses, the bewitching under-things that the Queen of the Fairies might wear, so delightfully gossamer-like are they. She steers her perambulator into groups of infuriated pedestrians; she rattles the bones of the infants not only over the stones of the sidewalk, but over many living toes and insteps and up sharply against human ankles. Elderly ladies will deliberately stop, and admonish and scold and threaten her. They demand the name of her mistress, in order that they may be enabled to lodge formal complaint against her. Betsinda cares little for all that. When the row is over she looks before her, and steers straight for some thirty seconds or so. Then her head turns on its axis again, her eyes gaze sideward. She is with the bonnets and the dresses once more, and with fearless faith she commits her precious burden to the care of the powers above.

If any one has not noticed this condition of facts, this curious distinction of classes, I can only pray him to open his eyes when next he makes his way through a crowded street in London, and then say whether my general observation is not correct. I suppose the philosophical explanation is not far to seek. The working man is hurrying to his work—he is tied to time. Betsinda has been sent out for a clearly-defined hour or two hours. The whistling errand-boy must get his errands done within at least plausible distance of punctuality and promptness. The young woman with the washing is already looked for here and there. These people cannot afford to lounge. If they have hurried past some sight that interests them they cannot quietly turn back, and composedly feast their eyes upon it. All they can do they do—and that is to keep looking sidewards or backwards, and retain it within their range of vision as long as they may, while still hurrying onward in the other direction—careless of collision, regardless of reproach. The boy, of course, is the most reckless of all. He will come rattling along the pavement at a hand-gallop, with his head positively twisted behind him like that of a professional contortionist. No matter what the risk to himself or to others, he will not lose sight of anything that amuses or interests him so long as his straining eyes in his contorted head can hold it within his perverse horizon. If he gets into a collision with some steady wayfarer he does not mind. Indeed, he considers it prime fun. The threats of an elderly gentleman have no terror for him; at the worst he can run much quicker than the elderly gentleman. For the admonitions of an elderly lady he has no ear. He interrupts her lecture, perhaps, by some disparaging remark upon her bonnet; possibly he asks her, with sudden affectation of friendly and intimate interest, "What price that?" He does not wait to hear what the cost of the article may have been, but plunges whistling on his way. The attempted admonition has done nothing but to make the elderly lady, her very self, an object of droll curiosity to him, and he now keeps his head twisted backward to enjoy as long as he can the sight of her bewilderment and her futile anger.

Do not ascend Ludgate Hill without bestowing a thought on Paternoster Row. Many an anxious heart has beat high as the owner and bearer of the heart paused in trepidation on the threshold of some house in the Row. To the young and timid author the place was holy ground. Many such aspirants must have felt inclined to put their somewhat broken shoes from off their feet in an effort at propitiation. The place is less distinctively, less exclusively, literary now than it was in former days. There are publishers now in Piccadilly and the Strand, and Oxford Street, and Albemarle Street,

ST. MARTIN'S, LUDGATE

and Burlington Street, and Covent Garden, and Cornhill, and many other places; but some of the greatest of publishing houses still hold on to the Row, and several newer houses have started life there. Talk of London ghosts—talk of haunted London— what region could be more ghost-frequented than Paternoster Row? The ghosts of all the literary projects which perished in their early youth; the novels, the poems, the essays, the volumes of travel, the translations, which died in Paternoster Row—which the public would not keep alive, which the world only too willingly let die! I should think that at every midnight there must be as many spectral forms in that gloomy lane as were gathered at the midnight review of the dead Napoleon in the German poem. I would go there some midnight to see, only for fear of one pale little ghost which I do not wish to meet: it is the ghost of a volume of translations from a foreign poet, at which I once toiled. Let it pass; let us speak no more of it. There was to me one comfort in its failure. No one knew anything about it. The reproach of the death fell not on my head. I name it not. As Béranger said of Waterloo, "Its name shall never sadden page of mine."

St Paul's! We are standing inside the great doorway which looks upon the statue of Queen Anne, and the railway bridge, and the crowd below. Few people who pass hurriedly by have any idea of the simplicity, the sympathy, the solemnity of that entrance —that porch. Mr. Pennell has put but a few—a very few—figures there. A young man stands on the threshold and looks down on the perpetual movement of the street. A girl is just about to go down the steps and plunge into the living stream. A man and woman have just come within the porch. They are strangers evidently; they look with awe, and move with reverential slowness. The man has already taken off his hat. Dr. Johnson would approve of him. The whole sketch admirably suggests the presence of a solemn sanctuary. It is a sanctuary — a sanctuary from the crowd, and the rush of business, and the struggle for money, and all the incarnate vulgarities of common daily life. It ought to do one's soul some good just to look up at that great temple as he passes on his way. Within all is quiet. No service is going on, but the organ is breathing, and there are a few listeners scattered here and there in the cool semi-darkness. St. Paul's is well placed—there in the very thick of the crowd and the traffic. It would show to more advantage, no doubt, if it were set upon an open plateau. I knew a dreamy man once who had a great ambition. He wanted to be rich, enormously rich, and for what do you think? That he might buy up all the houses round St. Paul's, and all the warehouses and wharves between it and the river, and clear them completely away, and allow the cathedral to stand revealed in all its proportions, isolated on a broad clear elevation above the Thames. My friend's was indeed an artistic and an exalted ambition. With what pride the Londoner—with what fresh delight and wonder the stranger—would see that dome and those walls rising uninterrupted, undisfigured, in full display above the Thames! Where in the heart of any great city would there be such another view of a grand cathedral? But, after all, is it not better as it is? Is not the place of such a cathedral more fittingly set in and amidst the crowd? The work of the pastor does not lie in picturesque and dignified solitude, but among the houses, and the cottages, and the garrets. I always think in this way of St. Paul's. Let it stand there with the waves of the world's traffic beating on its very steps. Some wayfarer may come ashore now and then and mount the steps, and enter the quiet and darkling church, and be reminded that the city is not all the world and all the worlds. I like to think of that dome rising high above all those roofs, and chimneys, and gables, and signs, and advertisements, and telegraph wires. I do not care to think of the whispering-gallery and the show-places of any kind, or even of the tomb of "the Duke" himself, or of any of the curious monuments in which half-draped personages from classic mythology pretend to be in grief over sturdy British soldiers and sailors. I do not care for the hum and drone of the verger explaining all about his sights. All that has, to my mind, nothing to do with the reality of St. Paul's. The mission of St. Paul's, to my thinking, is in its standing firmly planted there, in the very centre of the commonplace traffic, and bearing its silent testimony to other and greater realities. It stands and lifts its dome into the air, and its dome is surmounted by that Cross, which surely any creed or sect of men who are worshippers of anything may recognise to be, as this very Cross on St. Paul's was described in the last generation by a great parliamentary orator who was not of the English Church, "a sign of hope—a signal of salvation!"

VIII

ST. PAUL'S

WHAT a natural habit it is to personate into living and even into human form some inanimate object or structure with which one has become familiar and which is dear! No wonder that in the days of the Dryads people gave life and character and human sympathies to every tree and fountain and river which they had long known and which they loved. We nearly all find ourselves doing much the same sort of thing with buildings which we have long known, and which have grown to be in a certain sense a part of our existence. I always thus endow St. Paul's Cathedral with life and human nature and sympathy. I cannot well explain what early associations and chances have made St. Paul's a more living influence to me than the much grander and nobler Westminster Abbey; but so it is, and I feel as if St. Paul's were a living influence over all that region of the metropolis which is surveyed by its ball and its cross. But in another sense it is unlike other buildings to me. It is not one long-lived, long-lived cathedral; it is rather a generation of cathedrals. Westminster Abbey takes us back in unbroken continuity of history to the earlier days of England's budding greatness. Westminster itself, nevertheless, was only called so in the beginning to distinguish it from the earlier East Minster, which was either the existing St. Paul's or a cathedral standing on Tower Hill. It would seem, then, that St. Paul's rather than Westminster Abbey ought to represent the gradual movement of English history and English thought, and the growth of the metropolis. But observe the difference. Westminster Abbey has always, since its erection in the old days about the time when

Pan was definitely giving up the use of his Pagan horn, been sedately watching over London. It has been reconstructed here and there, of course—repaired and renovated, touched up and decorated with new adornments in tribute of grateful piety; but it is ever and always the same Westminster Abbey. Now observe the history of St. Paul's. St. Paul's has fallen and died time after time, and been revived and restored. It has risen new upon new generations. It has perished in flame again and again, like a succession of martyrs, and has come up afresh and with new-spangled ore flamed in the forehead of the morning sky. St. Paul's is a religious or ecclesiastical dynasty rather than a cathedral. It has been destroyed so often, and has risen again in so many different shapes, that it seems as if each succeeding age were putting its fresh stamp and mintmark on it, and so commending it to the special service of each new generation. One cannot but think that—let its authorities, its Dean and Chapter, and the rest, take all the best and most devoted care they can of it—St. Paul's is not destined to hold its present shape for a very long stretch of time. I do not desire my words to be like the story of the watchful and warned parent which is found in all literatures, from Æsop and the *Arabian Nights* downwards—the story of the father who is warned that an early death is impending over his dear and only son, and who locks the boy for greater security into a lofty tower or into a subterranean cavern—the tale is told in different ways—and behold it is all of no use, for the very precautions taken to save the lad only tend to his earlier and surer destruction. It may be thus with the Cathedral of St. Paul's. I hope the Dean and Chapter will not think me ill-omened with my prophecies of evil. I hope they will not feel to me as is usually felt by less considerate and enlightened persons towards even the well-intentioned who set out to warn and to alarm with forebodings of evil things to come. I have no warning to give, and therein I am no doubt less excusable than most of those who forecast sad troubles, for I cannot pretend to have any idea of what the danger is, or how it may be averted, or whence it is to arrive. I know nothing about it, and the Dean and Chapter themselves do not wish well to their noble Cathedral more cordially than I do. But I keep thinking of the past, and I cannot help murmuring to myself that the mission of St. Paul's is, as I have said, to be a succession or dynasty of cathedrals, and not to be one perennial structure with time-proof and fire-proof walls and an unbroken history.

This birth and re-birth give, to my thinking, an entirely peculiar interest to St. Paul's Cathedral. Think what its different generations could have told to all around! Another great church—Westminster Abbey, for example—grows up amid growing history, and is a part of its gradual movement, and so does not notice it. Each day makes its slight and almost imperceptible change, and the cathedral changes with the day, and is all-unconscious of it. Westminster Abbey could

ST. PAUL'S CHURCHYARD

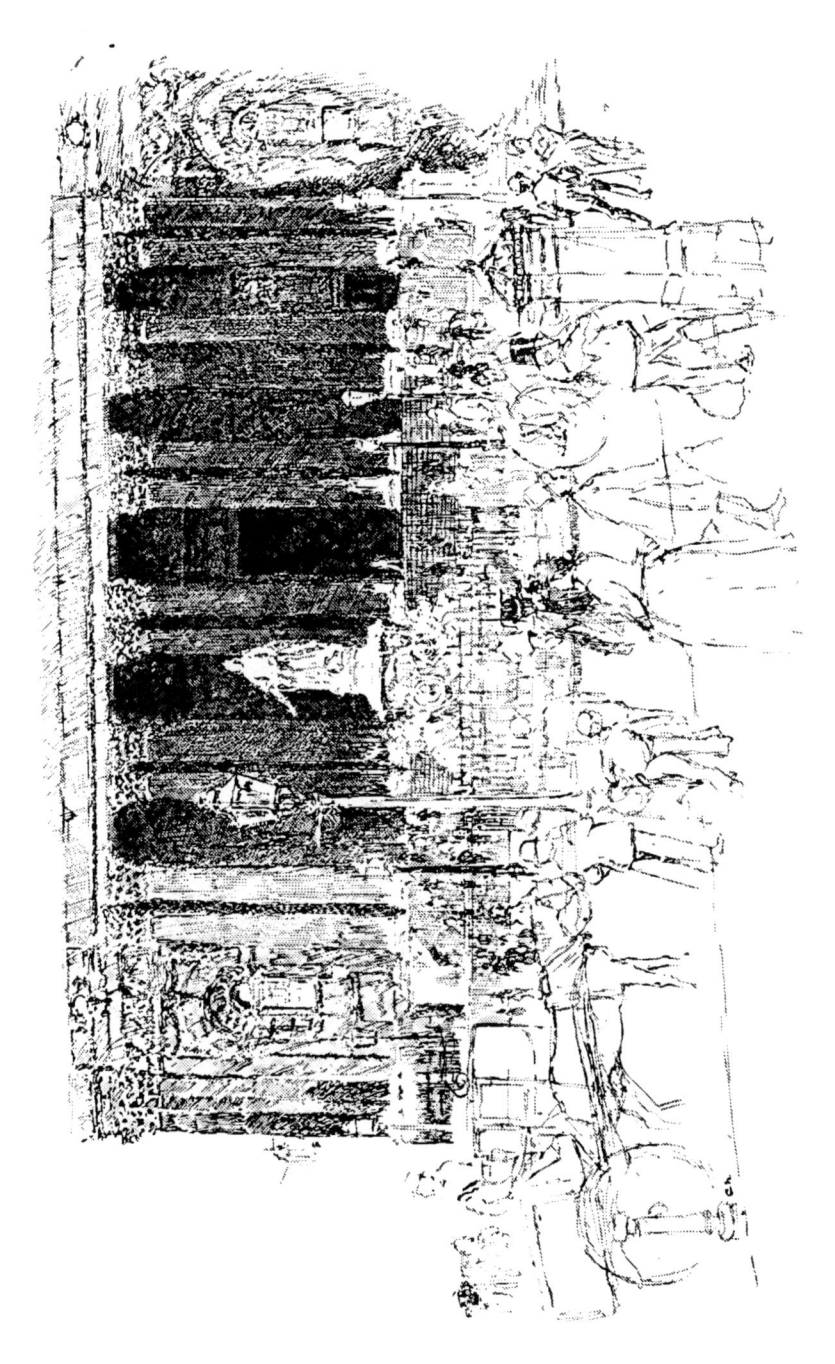

not tell how Roman dominion gradually faded, how Saxon gave place to Norman, and Tudor followed Plantagenet, and Stuart came to reign and to fade, and a new dynasty galloped in on the white horse of Hanover. One can imagine Westminster Abbey confusing new pageantry with old, the impressions of yesterday with the memories of centuries past, and hashing up the wedding of some mediæval prince with that of Mr. Henry M. Stanley. But St. Paul's, as we see it, was re-born into a world quite new to it only two centuries ago. It came then into new being with a quick re-born consciousness, taking fresh and eager notice of everything it saw. Above all, it could see and take account of change. "See here—and here—that was not so when I looked on this earth before! What has gone with this or that place, this or that dynasty, which I remember stout and flourishing only a hundred years ago or thereabouts?" Each revival means a new Hegira, a new point of comparison, a new standard of excellence, a new inspiration of sympathy; it may be a regret for the past, it may be a hope for the future. Thus St. Paul's has re-steeped, renewed again and again, its sentiments of companionship with humanity. St. Paul's is always young, that is, comparatively young—two centuries back to the last birth—that after the Great Fire; then another stretch to the former destruction and regeneration, and then back to another and another, until the first St. Paul's stands up in the raw dawn of London's history—always young, and yet enriched with the traditions, and much more than the traditions, the actual experiences, of centuries on centuries. This Cathedral, this generation of cathedrals, ought to be able to teach us lessons such as no English church endowed with a monotony of antiquity could well suggest.

That was a strange period of English history when the former St. Paul's Cathedral went into ashes amid the Great Fire of London. We can see that time through the eyes of two keen and shrewd observers, and never in the world were two contemporaneous observers less like to each other! How seriously and sternly Evelyn took everything! With what prosaic, matter-of-fact, ignoble tolerance Mr. Pepys took everything! Mr. Pepys would have listened with interest and a sort of platonic approval to Casanova's account of his amours, could he have lived to hear the narrative. He would not really have approved of such discourse or admired such a career. He would probably have told Mrs. Pepys in private what he thought of the pilgrim of erotic love, and he would certainly not have wished her to make the acquaintance of Casanova. But if Casanova happened to stand high in Court favour, we may be sure Mr. Pepys would have chanced the reputation of Mrs. Pepys and encouraged in her a friendly reception of the foreign blackguard. It would have been hard to get Evelyn to understand that there really could be a man like Casanova; but if he did get to understand him he would have allowed Casanova to know what he thought of him, and that without stint or measure. Never was in Court history a more stately, pure-souled gentleman than Evelyn—sweet, high-minded, high-cultured; a little cold, perhaps, a little over-fastidious, exacting too remorselessly from all humanity that austere morality which came naturally to himself—the Don Quixote of his day and his society, as Pepys assuredly was the Sancho Panza. Pepys was in his queer sort of way a moral man too; he would have been a very respectable man if he had lived in the days of George the Third and Dr. Johnson. Even as it was he certainly would have preferred moral men to rakes and libertines; but if the rakes and libertines were highly-placed courtiers he was not the person to weary and worry them by discoursing moral lessons; he would have thought it better form and more prudent to fall in with their talk and let it be supposed that he admitted a general approval of their ways and their principles of life—so far as they did not relate too directly to Mrs. Pepys. It was the destiny of these two men to record in personal memoirs their impressions of Court society about the time when St. Paul's was burnt down and rebuilt, and surely the world does not contain two such sincere and faithful pictures of the same scenes and the same age drawn with such different pencils and from such different points of view. The value of these books is beyond computation, and the value of one is immensely enhanced by the value of the other. I should like to set off two passages against each other. Take the few lines in which Pepys records the fact that he was permitted by a laundress or a waiting-maid, I think, to gaze upon Lady Castlemaine's laced petticoats and smocks, and his remark that it did his heart good to see those pretty and dainty garments. Take Evelyn's stern comment on the death of the King, and his picture of the scene in which not long before he had seen him surrounded by his favourite women and his riotous men companions, gaming and fooling, daffing the world aside and bidding it pass, in much more ignoble sense than Shakespeare ascribes to Harry the Prince of Wales and his gay and gallant comrades. "And now," Evelyn sums up, "is all in the dust!" Probably there was not a pin to choose between Evelyn's opinion of Lady Castlemaine and Pepys's—probably Pepys, in conversing with his wife of quiet evenings, described Lady Castlemaine in words which austere Evelyn would hardly have cared to repeat. But Pepys could do homage in public not only to Lady Castlemaine herself, but even to Lady Castlemaine's laced petticoats hanging on a line to dry. Evelyn scowled at vice even in the highest place, and pulled his hat upon his brows and went the other way; Evelyn would lose his life rather than bow down to Gessler's hat in the market-place. Pepys would willingly, if he were called upon, have done public homage in the market-place to the laced smock of Gessler's mistress exhibited on the top of a pole for the purpose of testing the loyal submissiveness of the community.

Evelyn has something direct and personal to do with the immediate subject on which we are engaged. When St. Paul's was burnt, Evelyn was appointed one of the Commissioners for its rebuilding. The same event, by the way, threw increased cares upon Pepys, for he was what we should now call Secretary to the Admiralty; and the Plague, the Fire of London, and the Dutch in the Medway and the Thames, occupied much of the attention of Pepys's official superiors for three successive years, and devolved the business of the Admiralty Department almost altogether upon him. Pepys and Evelyn both lived to see, or at least both might have seen, the public opening of the choir of Sir Christopher Wren's new cathedral. Neither lived to see the completion of the whole structure, with its dome proudly surmounting London. Evelyn outlived Pepys by two or three years; the chances are that in literature Pepys may outlive Evelyn.

Was there ever known in the history of the world and its churches any cathedral which suffered from fire like St. Paul's? The whole career of the church was an ordeal by fire. It was injured by fire a hundred years before Westminster Hall was built; it was totally destroyed by fire in the eleventh century, and it took nearly two centuries to restore it to anything like its former magnificence. "Away! we lose ourselves in light," might have been its motto, for it was all but completely destroyed by fire in the fifteenth century, and its spire, which then claimed to be the highest in the world, was destroyed by fire a century later. Thus, we have brought it to the terrible days of 1666, when it went under with so much of London to accompany it—one of the most tremendous conflagrations recorded in the history of great cities. Then came the Commission to rebuild it, of which brave John Evelyn was a member, and then Sir Christopher Wren raised the monument to his fame, which those who would question his renown have only to look upon and be satisfied. The great architect sleeps within the shelter of the Cathedral which he raised up out of dust and ashes, and never was simpler, nobler, or juster epitaph inscribed on the tomb of man than that which commends his remains to the reverence of the world. The Great Fire of 1666 was but an accident in the architectural career of Sir Christopher Wren. He had in any case been appointed, long before the fire, one of the Commission to consider and report upon the entire rebuilding of the Cathedral, which had been put together in a patchy sort of way, one man's notion of architectural beauty and fitness overriding rather than supplementing another. For a long time it had been resolved to obtain symmetry, cohesion, and consistency in the building, and it had at length begun to make itself manifest that such an object could only be obtained by the pulling down of the old structure, and the erection of a new cathedral which should be designed by the intellect and the imagination of one man, the creation of one exalted intellect. But the scheme got pushed aside by one interference and another. Politics interfered; hostility and rival schemes interfered; mere delay and vague postponement interfered; and it seemed likely that nothing would be done. The Great Fire came to the rescue and ordained that something should be done. Even then Wren did not have it all his own way—what man of genius ever had whose lot it was to be controlled by what is called the practical mind? For example, Wren's idea was to adopt a principle such as that which I spoke of lately as having become an aspiration in the mind of a friend of mine— the principle that St. Paul's should stand in clear isolation, and be seen along the river from its dome to its base. It was in the mind of Wren that this should be accomplished by making a long line of stately quays to border the Thames—by anticipating, in fact, and carrying out farther down the stream the idea of the Thames Embankment. But Wren was not allowed to put this plan into action. Houses, warehouses, and wharves were permitted to crowd anyway they would

WEST DOOR OF ST. PAUL'S

around the base of the Cathedral, and St. Paul's stood as we see it standing now—or rather it stood then and stands now as nobody can see it, except in glimpses and portions and instalments. Still, we may, if we will, make some poetic association even out of its present eclipsed and occulted condition to add to that consideration which I have already offered, that the neglect and error of past generations has left St. Paul's to have its base in the very heart of the City's life. Is it not also like some vast and stately tree, some great cedar, some lofty palm, some majestic outgrowth of a Sacramento forest, which lifts its head and spreads its broad branches away in the clear upper air, and has the lowly brushwood, and the green mosses, and the wild flowers, and the poor, lowly, common weeds around its base?

Edmund Burke, if I am not mistaken, once had an idea that the dome of St. Paul's should be gilded over, and should thus flame in burnished splendour across the city like some golden-roofed palace in the *Arabian*

Nights. The magnificence of the idea was worthy of the mind of Burke. But in that idea, as in others, Burke reckoned without his public and without his conditions. How glorious it would look, that golden dome, lighted up by the morning sky or burning in the sunset—while the gilding was new! But how would it be when the gilding began to get old and tarnished, when the thick rain of the City had blackened it as with marking-ink, when the grime of the City smoke had settled on it, and when only dim, defaced patches here and there reminded the gazer that the dome had ever borne a surface of shining gold? The gilding could be renewed, it may be said. Yes, it could be renewed; of course it could be renewed. But would it have been renewed without delay? Is it thus we find that things are managed in the City and in all other communities? Would there not be delay and debate and objection? Would there not be apathy and counter-project? Would there not be disparaging suggestion, and questions of economy and of a cheaper contract and a less costly style of gilding—yellow ochre, perhaps, or gamboge, laid dexterously on to look as well, or nearly as well—as well in a manner—as Mr. Burke's too expensive style of ornamentation? Then the gilt of the dome would meanwhile begin to look shabby, and thoughtless folk would gibe at it, and the dome which Burke revered would become the laughing-stock for men—of whom there were always a few—who had not exactly the intellect or the culture of Burke. And Burke, too, who had read his Shakespeare and appreciated him, to have made such a proposition! Had he forgotten that often-quoted line from "Troilus and Cressida" in which Ulysses tells us that "One touch of nature makes the whole world kin"? Never have I seen that line quoted—and I meet with the quotation seven times a-week on an average —without seeing from the way in which it is introduced that he who quotes it fondly and firmly believes the words are used to touch the heart by exalting the common qualities of human nature. Alas! the kinship of which Ulysses speaks is a different sort of thing—it is the kinship of ignoble, mean, and grovelling instinct. The very illustration Ulysses uses explains my allusion to Burke's forgetfulness in not taking the lesson of those lines, when he talked about gilding the dome of St. Paul's. What is the touch of nature that makes the whole world kin? According to Ulysses, wise in his own conceit and truly in the conceit of others, it is the "one consent" with which mankind

> "Give to dust that is a little gilt
> More laud than gilt o'er-dusted."

Would not this touch of nature have asserted its sway over the average public of London as they passed up and down the river, mounted and descended Ludgate Hill, tramped through Cheapside eastward and westward, and saw Burke's gilding on St. Paul's dome o'er-dusted by the unadorning and irreverent incense coming up night and day from the pavements of the City? How much of reverence would remain for Burke's splendid idea when the dome was growing every day more dusty and grimy? How many men would see the idea beneath the dust? How many men would fail to prefer any new garnish and glittering sight, any "new-born gawd," any dust that was a little gilded, to Burke's thought of the golden dome? How many men would not prefer the outward show of a piece of gilt gingerbread? It was lucky that no one really thought of carrying out Burke's plan. Burke himself has declared, in a passage full of most melancholy and unquestionable truth, that no human system can come to good which is based on the heroic virtues. It is of no avail to think of keeping up some system which is only to be kept up on condition that we are all and always heroic. So of the fine project for the gilding of the dome of St. Paul's. If gilt would only never tarnish, if smoke would for ever refuse to begrime a golden dome, if men would always repair at once the damages of weather and of dirt, if other men would be magnanimous enough to see a great idea under an occasional clouding of dust—then that gilded dome might have been a grand success. But smoke is smoke and soot is soot, and men will gibe and see the ridiculous side of everything—or what is to them the ridiculous side—and Ulysses' touch of nature makes the whole world kin, and it is well that St. Paul's dome has been left ungilded.

The night comes, and St. Paul's is alone. All that part of the City which approaches it and environs it is now without movement and life. No lights burn along Ludgate Hill. The statue of Queen Anne peers down that way into darkness. No windows gleam in Cheapside. Bow Bells chime out after midnight to mere solitude. There is something particularly melancholy, inane, and futile in the thought of a bell pealing out its notes without even the chance to awaken sleeping ears. No one lives in that part of the City. That part of the City has gone home to bed. It has gone to bed in Park

Lane and Piccadilly, and Belgrave Square and Eaton Square; in Norwood and Hampstead and Clapham; in Wood Green and Brondesbury; in Bethnal Green and Stratford-atte-Bow; down along the line of docks; anywhere: that City population takes in all the ranks and classes of life. The Asmodeus who could study the sleeping accommodation of all the City folk who fly the neighbourhood of St. Paul's after dark, would have rare opportunity for easy satire over the social diversities of condition in London. Supposing he were a good-natured demon, admitting in him a certain sympathy for man's distracted condition between tempting possibilities and cramping limitations, what would be the outcome of his survey—despondency or hope?

Anyhow, the space around St. Paul's is silent, clear, and lonely. The living have gone. Then, perhaps, do the dead come back and take their old places? Does a Restoration crowd stream round the base of the Cathedral and admire it as it has risen from its ruins? Does Charles himself come with his gipsy complexion and his dark love-locks? Does Nell Gwynn come smirking there? and do Evelyn and Pepys arrive arm-in-arm? Grim Prince Rupert, turned chemist and chemical toy-maker in his older days, the time quite gone when he could win his half of any battle, is he there? Has that greatest man of his day, surpassing man of any day, come from his ship-carpenter work on Tower Hill, and from his drinks of brandy with pepper in it—has Peter the Czar of Russia, Peter the Great, wandered westward to look up to the dome of St. Paul's? It would be curious to think whether this revisiting of the glimpses of the moon around St. Paul's is limited or not to the company of those who saw the latest resurrection of the Cathedral, or whether the spectres from all time or nearly so, going back to the days of Roman sentinels, may appear of nights on Ludgate Hill, and do honour to the latest edition of St. Paul's. On that question I can venture no opinion. But I am firm in the conviction that the Cathedral is never left quite alone. The living surround it in the day; the dead are free of it in the night. The Monument is the contemporary of its latest birth. Westminster Abbey is too young to have been the contemporary of its first appearance on its eastern hill.

THE END

Printed by R. & R. CLARK, *Edinburgh.*

BIBLIOLIFE

Old Books Deserve a New Life
www.bibliolife.com

Did you know that you can get most of our titles in our trademark **EasyScript**™ print format? **EasyScript**™ provides readers with a larger than average typeface, for a reading experience that's easier on the eyes.

Did you know that we have an ever-growing collection of books in many languages?

Order online:
www.bibliolife.com/store

Or to exclusively browse our **EasyScript**™ collection:
www.bibliogrande.com

At BiblioLife, we aim to make knowledge more accessible by making thousands of titles available to you – quickly and affordably.

Contact us:
BiblioLife
PO Box 21206
Charleston, SC 29413

LaVergne, TN USA
27 November 2009

165415LV00004B/6/P